Leadership
for Equity and
Excellence

Foreword by Carl D. Glickman

Leadership for Equity and Excellence

Creating High-Achievement Classrooms, Schools, and Districts

James Joseph Scheurich
Linda Skrla

CORWIN PRESS, INC.
A Sage Publications Company
Thousand Oaks, California

CATALOGUED

For information:

Corwin Press, Inc.
A Sage Publications Company
2455 Teller Road
Thousand Oaks, California 91320
www.corwinpress.com

Sage Publications Ltd.
6 Bonhill Street
London EC2A 4PU
United Kingdom

Sage Publications India Pvt. Ltd.
B-42, Panchsheel Enclave
Post Box 4109
New Delhi 110 017 India

Printed in the United States of America

Library of Congress Cataloging-in-Publication Data

Scheurich, James Joseph, 1944-
Leadership for equity and excellence: Creating high-achievement classrooms, schools, and districts / James Joseph Scheurich, Linda Skrla.
    p. cm.
Includes bibliographical references and index.
ISBN 978-0-7619-4585-7 (cloth)
ISBN 978-0-7619-4586-4 (pbk.)
    1. Educational equalization-United States. 2. Academic achievement-United States. I. Skrla, Linda, 1957- II. Title.
LC213.2 .S36 2003
379.2'6—dc21

                        2002154806

This book is printed on acid-free paper.

09 10 11 12 11 10 9 8 7 6 5

Acquisitions Editor:	Robert D. Clouse
Associate Editor:	Kristen L. Gibson
Editorial Assistant:	Jingle Vea
Production Editor:	Denise Santoyo
Typesetter:	C&M Digitals (P) Ltd.
Indexer:	Kay Dusheck
Cover Designer:	Tracy E. Miller

Contents

Foreword

For many years now, I have greatly admired the work of Jim Scheurich and Linda Skrla. This book, *Leadership for Equity and Excellence*, reaffirms for me why. With passion, wisdom, and perseverance, they challenge all of us as educators to examine our beliefs, attitudes, and practices about the students in our charge. Professors Scheurich and Skrla make clear that there should be only one agenda for every classroom, school, and district in America, and that agenda must be driven by the single belief that equity and excellence are the same. All our students—regardless of culture, race, ethnicity, economics, language, gender, or lifestyle—must be educated to attain well-defined and high standards of learning. To have any other agenda or to do anything less perpetuates a public educational system that expects more of some students, mainly white and of wealth, than of other students, mainly of color, in poverty, or both.

What sets this book apart from other writings about school leadership and successful schools is the authors' unflinching appraisal that there is great hope, in the midst of great hypocrisy, that American schools can narrow and eventually eliminate the achievement gap. The authors have personally studied schools and districts that have, over time, created educational methods, programs, and expectations that have significantly advanced the educational achievements of all students. No longer are the highest achieving students in these schools only those who are traditionally expected to do well, and no longer are special needs programs filled with students typically viewed as "high risk" due to their poverty, language, race, or ethnicity.

The authors are correct in pointing out that although most educators easily mouth the words "All children can learn," relatively few educators have endeavored to study and change the very practices that keep all children from actually doing so. This book is a ray of sunshine through the fog of complacency among those who think that we are doing the best that we can for poor students and students of color. The complacent might think that classrooms and schools can help produce an exceptional student or two who rises above his or her underachieving group, but such educators rarely think that these gains can be made across the board in the same proportion as is the case among the "good" students from middle- and upper-class backgrounds with college-educated parents.

Scheurich and Skrla shake the environmental or genetic rationale about educational attainment to its hollow core and go beyond exhortations into explaining what schools can do. They provide chapter after chapter of easily understood strategies drawn from examples of classrooms, schools, and districts that have already greatly improved. The authors demonstrate how leaders in such schools mobilize faculty, staff, and community to openly study inequities among students, and how standards, curriculum, and assessments are used as levers for identifying and improving student achievement. The authors describe how leaders promote purposeful and collaborative classrooms among teachers, administrators, and parents to improve instruction, create with others a climate of care, and use accountability and "equity audits" to continuously scan for inequities across multiple domains of student learning and activities.

Jim Scheurich and Linda Skrla are independent thinkers. They kowtow to no political or ideological group. One is hard pressed to categorize them as politically left or right or educationally progressive or conservative. Where else do you find authors who argue forcefully for clear academic standards, tests, and assessments, for curriculum alignment, and for accountability, who at the same time argue equally hard for collaborative and flexible ways for determining instructional practices, and who vent with moral indignation against "teaching to the test" and using classrooms and schools as "testing factories"?

This text is not "pie in the sky" theoretical conjecture but an examination of real people in real schools who will no longer tolerate inequities of achievement in their own classrooms, schools, districts, and communities. This book is both eloquent in its simplicity and deeply moving in its call to action. When I read this book, I can hear the evocative strains of Ron Edmonds' effective schools research combined with the heroes and heroines of the women's suffrage, child labor, and civil rights movements. I hear the challenge of those, known and unknown to us, who had the courage and stamina to turn the tide of how humans think about each other.

Myles Horton (1998, p. 114) wrote, "A large social movement forces people to take a stand for or against it, so that there are no longer any neutrals." Jim Scheurich and Linda Skrla, with so many others who have pushed forward the equity and excellence movement in education, are clearly, and once again, asking each educator to take a stance—no more neutrals allowed. Do you believe that all children can learn? Do you believe that all children can learn to high predetermined standards? If you say that you *do* believe, or are at least willing to consider such a creed about the educability of all humans, then take this book with you. It will provide you with a world of practice—drawn from schools, faculty, and leaders who make the belief the practice of their work. Over and over again, this is a book whose time has come.

—Carl D. Glickman
Professor and Roy F. and
Joann Cole Endowed Chair
College of Education
Southwest Texas State University

REFERENCE

Horton, M. (1998). *The long haul: An autobiography*. New York: Teachers College Press.

Acknowledgments

The Sid W. Richardson Foundation of Fort Worth, Texas, funded the research project upon which much of this book is based. The board of directors and Executive Director Valleau Wilkie, Jr. have our deepest appreciation for their generous support and for their commitment to improving education for literally all children.

Jim's Acknowledgments

Thanks to Patti Spencer for her unwavering love and support.

Thanks to my totally beloved children, Corinna and Jasper, who always sit in the center of my heart.

Thanks to my mom and dad, Bea and Jim, for raising me, for continuing to love me no matter how far I strayed.

Thanks to Linda Skrla for being such a wonderful partner in this book and in all of the great work we have done together. If the Goddess were creating a perfect friend, colleague, and coauthor for me, it would be Linda. We have walked an exciting, satisfying, and meaningful path together. Yes, sometimes there were brambles on the path, but the mutual, loving commitment to each other and to the school children we happily serve always carried us through to a better place. Thank you, Linda, for all of it.

Thanks to all the school children who have inspired me, who have taught me, who have brought me onto this holy path. Special thanks to those south side urban children in my very first school who taught me a thousand times more than I taught them. They were the ones who taught me how deeply my country was failing to love all its children and how strongly our public educational system needed to be equitable and just. In many ways, they were my beginning.

Thanks to Jay Scribner for always being so caring and supportive.

Thanks to Pedro Reyes, Lonnie Wagstaff, Bill Moore, and John Roueche for mentoring me.

Thanks to Martha Ovando, Don Phelps, and Michael Thomas for supporting me as the junior professor in their midst.

Thanks to Peter Wheat for his constant help, his wonderful personality, his music, and his friends.

Thanks to Sarah Jimenez for always, always being perfectly perfect.

Thanks to Pam Clinger for all of her hard work and support, while always maintaining the best spirit.

Thanks to all my students at the University of Texas at Austin; you have been a constant source of inspiration. I truly believe you are the future of education, and what a fine future it is.

Linda's Acknowledgments

My thanks and my love go first to my family. My husband Steve, who is a school administrator out there on the front lines living daily the struggles that I research and write about, and my sons, Steve, Scott, and Eric, are my abiding sources of love and support.

I also deeply appreciate my college and department colleagues at Texas A&M for their collegiality and support as I have learned my way in academia. My dean, Jane Close Conoley, my department head, Bryan Cole, along with Yvonna Lincoln, David Erlandson, Carolyn Clark, Patrick Slattery, Christine Stanley, John Hoyle, Jean Madsen, Carol Patitu, Luana Zellner, Virginia Collier, Arnold Oates, Steve Stark, Cliff Whetten, Maynard Bratlien, Stan Carpenter, Bob

Slater, Julian Trevino, and Dean Corrigan, have been a wonderfully nurturing group with whom to work.

Thanks go as well to the outstanding students in our department, especially my two superlative graduate assistants, Dawn Hogan and Ana Maria Sierra, doctoral students (now graduates) Toni Riester, Vickie Pursch, and Lezley Lewis, and master's student Ed Fellows.

I am indebted to several people from the University of Texas at Austin, where I completed my doctoral studies. I am deeply grateful to my dissertation advisor, Pedro Reyes, for his teaching and mentoring and for his unswerving belief in my ability to be a scholar. I also appreciate the friendship and support of fellow UT student Michelle Young. Additional thanks go to the Cycle XI and Cycle XII fellows of the Cooperative Superintendency Program for being an extended and consistent network of support. I particularly appreciate the friendship of Judi Benestante, Nic Retana, Glenn Nolly, Chon Garza, Jane Owen, Ron Peace, Andrea Rorrer, and Jennifer Scott.

Thanks also to several courageous individuals who took on the challenge of mentoring an often prickly and difficult beginning teacher, then assistant principal, and then curriculum director. These people include Ann Walsingham, Larry Wadzeck, and Paul Clore.

Finally, heartfelt thanks and deepest appreciation go to Jim Scheurich. He is a brilliant scholar, a world-class mentor, a simpatico coauthor, and a cherished friend. Our work together has, quite literally, changed my life, and it is my sincerest hope that Jim's and my collaborative work, in small or large ways, will change positively the lives of children, teachers, and leaders in schools serving low-income communities and communities of color.

Jim and Linda's Acknowledgments

We'd like to thank the research team on the project from which many of the recommendations we make in this book come—Joe Johnson, Jim Koschoreck, Dawn Hogan, and Pam Smith. Thanks also to the students and staff in the four districts who participated in our research—Aldine ISD, Brazosport ISD, San Benito CISD, and Wichita Falls ISD.

Our thanks to Juanita Garcia and Glenn Nolly for working with us to develop the "equity audits" discussed in one of the chapters. They are truly wonderful colleagues whom we love working with. Also, our special thanks go to Kathryn McKenzie for reading and commenting upon the manuscript for this book.

Our thanks to Robb Clouse at Corwin Press for his insightful and excellent editorial work.

In addition, Corwin Press gratefully acknowledges the contributions of the following reviewers:

Deborah A. Drugan
Principal, General John J. Stefanik Elementary School
Chicopee, MA

Dr. Suzanne Gilmour
Associate Professor and Chair, Educational
    Administration
State University of New York, Oswego
Oswego, NY

Sheryl Goffman
Principal, West Haverstraw Elementary School
West Haverstraw, NY

Dr. Wendy A. Harriott
Assistant Professor of Education, School of Education
Monmouth University, West Long Branch, NJ

Dr. Judith Frank-Gonwa
Assistant Professor, Westcott School
Northbrook, IL

About the Authors

James Joseph Scheurich is Associate Professor in Educational Administration and the director of the Public School Executive Leadership Programs at the University of Texas at Austin. His doctorate was earned at Ohio State University. He is the author of two books, *Anti-Racist Scholarship* (2002) and *Research Method in the Postmodern* (1997), and coauthor with Bob Donmoyer and Michael Imber of *The Knowledge Base in Educational Adminis-tration* (1995). In addition, he and Linda Skrla are the authors of the forthcoming book *Equity and Accountability*. He is the coeditor with Angela Valenzuela of the journal *International Journal of Qualitative Studies in Education*. He is the author or coauthor of numerous articles in academic journals, including *Educational Researcher*, *Journal of Education Policy*, *Urban Education*, *Educational Administration Quarterly*, *Education and Urban Society*, and the *International Journal of Leadership in Education*, among others. He also writes newspaper editorials and for educator journals, such as *Phi Delta Kappan*.

Linda Skrla is Assistant Professor in the Educational Administration and Human Resource Development Department at Texas A&M University. She holds a Ph.D. from the University of Texas at Austin, where she was a Cycle XI fellow of the Cooperative Super-intendency Program. Prior to joining the Texas A&M faculty in 1997, Skrla worked for

14 years as a middle school and high school teacher and as a campus and district administrator in public schools. Her research focuses on educational equity issues in school leadership, including accountability, high-success districts, and women superintendents. She is coauthor of *The Emerging Principalship* (2001) and coeditor of the forthcoming *Reconsidering Feminist Research in Educational Leadership*. Her published work has appeared in numerous journals, including *Educational Researcher*, *Educational Administration Quarterly*, *Phi Delta Kappan*, *Journal of School Leadership*, *Journal of Education Policy*, and the *International Journal of Qualitative Studies in Education*.

CHAPTER ONE

Working on the Dream

I have a dream that one day this nation will rise up and live out the true meaning of its creed: "We hold these truths to be self-evident: that all men are created equal." . . . I have a dream that my four children will one day live in a nation where they will not be judged by the color of their skin but by the content of their character.

—Martin Luther King, Jr. (1963),
U.S. civil rights leader

This book is based on research we have done, on research others have done, and on our experiences in our own careers as educators. The goal of this book is to provide advice for school leaders and educators who want to develop schools that are both equitable *and* excellent. By equitable and excellent, we mean schools in which literally all students achieve high levels of academic success, regardless of any student's race, ethnicity, culture, neighborhood, income of parents, or home language.

For us, leadership for equity and excellence is a call for educators to continue to work on achieving the "dream" that

Martin Luther King referred to in his famous "I Have a Dream" speech. This speech was delivered on the steps of the Lincoln Memorial in Washington, D.C., on August 28, 1963. In this speech, Dr. King said,

> I say to you today, my friends, that in spite of the difficulties and frustrations of the moment, I still have a dream. It is a dream deeply rooted in the American dream. I have a dream that one day this nation will rise up and live out the true meaning of its creed: "We hold these truths to be self-evident: that all men are created equal."

In education, as in other areas of our social life, the dream that Martin Luther King was referring to—the dream for equity in our country—has not yet been achieved. However, "in spite of the difficulties and frustrations of the moment," it is extremely important that we continue to hold fast to this dream, that we continue to work hard to make it come true in education. That is what this book is about. It is about how to create schools in which the dream of equity comes alive on an every day basis through the work of ordinary, everyday people, just like you and us.

In striving for both equity *and* excellence, we are aiming to create schools in which virtually all students are learning at high academic levels. We are aiming for schools in which there are no persistent patterns of differences in academic success or treatment among students grouped by race, ethnicity, culture, neighborhood, income of parents, or home language. In other words, we are aiming to foster schools that literally serve each and every student really well.

Let us illustrate what we mean. Suppose you are the principal or a teacher in an elementary or secondary school serving children who are diverse by race, income of parents, culture, home language, and so forth. Suppose almost all of your students are at or above grade level in their academic achievement. Suppose your school achieved this not by drill and kill, not by becoming a test prep factory (i.e., spending the whole school year teaching to a state accountability test), but by having staff, parents, and students work together to learn how children in your school can be successfully taught.

Thus, in your school, the middle-class children do not do better academically than the children of low-income parents. The white children do not do better than the children of color. In your school, virtually all children achieve at high levels, and there is no discernable difference in academic success among different groups of students. Your school, in short, is what we mean by an equitable and excellent school.

However, we understand that many people, including educators and school leaders, do not believe that such schools are possible. We know this. We run into it constantly as we speak in various venues all across the country. Many, many people—including university scholars, campus and district administrators, and classroom teachers—just don't believe it is possible to create schools that are both equitable and excellent.

This disbelief, this resistance to the very possibility of equity, reminds us of many other situations in which, at first, people did not believe that something was possible, but then some people decided that it was; they then did "the impossible," eventually making the achievement ordinary. Not too long ago, many people believed that women could not succeed in college and become doctors, lawyers, jet pilots, or CEOs of major corporations, but women hold all of these positions today (certainly not as commonly as we would want, but more commonly than before).

Not too long ago, if you had told people that in less than ten years something like the Internet would exist and that people all over the world would routinely use it, people would have said you had been watching too much *Star Trek*. Similarly, not too long ago, many people did not believe that any child of color could be at the top of his or her class, but today this happens frequently, and it happens in some of the best schools in the country. At some point, people decide that they can succeed at what others had commonly, firmly believed was not possible—and they figure out how to do so. In fact, it seems like we spend much too much time saying that we can't do something or that it is too hard, when human history is full of examples of people creating new things that change the way we all think and change society as a whole.

We would like to suggest, then, that we as educators are spending too much time resisting the possibility that we can create both equitable and excellent schools. We would like to suggest that this limited way of thinking is not the truth; it is just a currently common social belief that can be changed. We would like to suggest that if educators would stop this resistance, stop saying that we can't create such schools and, instead, decide that we can, then we could use our time and energy to figure out how to do so.

We can be just as creative as anyone else. We can come up with new ideas, new ways of accomplishing educational success. We *know* that we can figure out how to create schools that are both equitable and excellent.

We may have to see that our beliefs and attitudes are partly the cause of some of the problems. We may have to see that we have some biases that are hurting children. We may have to take a tough look at some things we would rather not look at. However, we deeply, strongly, emphatically believe that together we can do this.

Why do we believe this? First, we believe that "can't" is the most destructive verb in an educator's vocabulary. New ideas, creative possibilities, important transformations, great changes—none of these emerge out of "can't."

Second, we believe that educators are some of the finest people in the world. We are not trying to put any other group of people down. We are just saying that there is not a better group of people in our society. Virtually all educators are driven by a strong desire to serve children. Educators know the importance of education to our children's futures and our country's future. Educators work as hard as or harder than anyone else. We take everyone's children, and we do the best we possibly can to educate all of them. If we were going to pick a group to lead society in a major step forward toward improving equity in our society, we would choose educators. Not all of us are great, but we are an excellent group upon which to build an exceptional future, an equitable future.

Third, in our work and research, we have repeatedly seen and studied many classrooms, schools, and districts that are both equitable and excellent. We know from direct, personal, and extensive experience that equitable and excellent schools are possible. We also know that schools like these are not just created by a few exceptional people. We know that ordinary, everyday people, just like you and us, have developed and can develop equitable and excellent schools.

Fourth, although it was the right thing to do all along, creating schools that are both equitable and excellent is now virtually a necessity due to quickly changing demographics. The race and ethnicity demographics of this country are changing very rapidly, faster than even many demographers expected. Students of color already dominate our largest cities, where most of our people live, and are rapidly expanding into all the suburbs and exurbs. All of the largest states—New York, Florida, California, Texas, Illinois (where, together, 40% of our population lives)—already have or will soon have students of color as the majority. For example, the majority of students in Texas schools are already children of color, and by about 2020, two-thirds of the entire Texas population will be people of color. One of every two children in Texas public schools participates in the federal free or reduced-price lunch program, and one in every seven children has limited English proficiency. The other large states are on a similar trajectory.

This means that high percentages of the new worker population already are young women and men of color. This, in turn, means the economy, especially of the large states (which have a disproportionate influence on the national economy), will soon be directly dependent on how successful we are in educating children of color. In other words, the success of our society will soon be directly dependent on our ability as educators to be successful with children of color, with whom we have not been very successful in the past. Consequently, if we want our society to move forward in a positive way, both socially and economically, we must become much more successful with children of color than we have been to date. We explicitly have no other choice.

Fifth, creating equitable, excellent schools has unquestionably been the right thing to do from the beginning. This is the point of what Dr. Martin Luther King was talking about. We must all work hard to realize the dream. We must make it come true. We say we live in a democracy; we say we are proud of our democracy; we say the rest of the world ought to have democracy, too, but inequity by race, ethnicity, culture, home language, and so forth exists in our schools. This inequity directly undermines our claim to be an exemplary democracy. In response, we are suggesting that it is we educators who must make the dream of an equitable democracy come true. Educators today *are*, as Robert Moses (Moses & Cobb, 2002) suggested, the frontline civil rights workers in a long-term struggle that started with the birth of this country. Decade by decade, people have fought to increase equity for people of color, for people with different cultures and home languages, and for people in low-income families.

Today, this fight, this struggle, this civil rights work has come to us as educators. Rather than walking in demonstrations or doing sit-ins at lunch counters or being arrested for our beliefs, we must carry forth this civil rights struggle on a day-to-day basis in single classrooms and single schools in every state.

This exalted work, this great and wonderful struggle, has been handed to us. It is not a burden, it is a gift. It is a true gift that we are in this place at this time. It is a gift to be an important part of something that is highly valuable, that has tremendous implications for society.

We honor those who participated in the great changes of the past in this country. We honor Martin Luther King and the civil rights workers. We honor César Chávez and the civil rights workers who stood beside him in his efforts for migrant workers. We honor all the men and women who have stood up and made our society better, who have increased the dignity, value, and equity of all people. Now, it is *we* who must become those same kinds of people. It is up to us to carry the great dream to fruition.

Sixth, this is spiritually the right thing to do. Virtually all people believe that we are all created equal. Virtually all religions believe that we are equally the children of God or the Great Spirit or the Creator or whatever word, name, or phrase you prefer. It is very simple: If you believe in spirituality, you can't believe that inequity by race, ethnicity, social class, culture, or home language is acceptable. Personally, we believe that it is our spiritual duty as educators to create schools that are equitable; schools that serve literally all children really well; schools that respect, appreciate, care for, and love each and every child.

To summarize, then, our reasons for creating schools that are both equitable and excellent are the following: First, "can't" is not allowed; together we can figure this problem out; it *is* a challenge we can meet. Second, we as educators are the people, the new civil rights workers, who can bring this dream to fruition. Third, we have seen and researched schools that are equitable and excellent, and, thus, we know that ordinary, everyday people, just like you and us, can accomplish this. Fourth, our changing demographics demand that we accomplish this if we want a successful national future, both economically and socially. Fifth, creating a truly equitable democracy is the right thing to do. It is the fulfillment of democracy. Sixth, spiritually, we have a sacred duty to accomplish this work.

WHAT WE WILL COVER IN THE BOOK

The next chapter, Chapter 2, is about vision and beliefs. It focuses on learning to believe in the possibility of creating schools that are both equitable and excellent, and it explores the barriers to believing this. Chapter 3 covers standards and curriculum. More specifically, the focus in this chapter is on the use of standards and curriculum in providing leadership for equity and excellence.

Chapter 4 is on instruction and classroom climate. However, the purpose of the chapter is not to provide detailed "how-to" instructions on various techniques, like collaborative grouping. There are plenty of good books and articles that already do that. Instead, we focus simultaneously on some areas that we think teachers are not getting sufficient exposure to and practices that we have found to be particularly important to creating equitable and excellent schooling. Nonetheless, even in these latter areas, we do not provide detailed instructions. Rather, we try to provoke your thinking and to include some readings to get you started on other resources.

Chapter 5 focuses on accountability and appropriate use of data. Chapter 6 covers systemic inequities and using data to uncover and erase them. Chapter 7 is about school leadership and its constant improvement. Chapter 8 focuses on what we call "proactive redundancy." Chapter 9 centers on parents, community, and context. Chapter 10 is our final call to everyone—including ourselves.

Our primary goal, as we seek to create schools that are both equitable and excellent, is to serve all of our children really well, regardless of their differences. We want to help create outstanding schools in which virtually all children are highly successful. We think any goal that is less than this sells our children short, sells ourselves short, and sells short the dream for a truly equitable society.

CHAPTER TWO

Learning to Believe the Dream Is Possible

We hold these truths to be self-evident, that all men are created equal, that they are endowed by their Creator with certain unalienable Rights, that among these are Life, Liberty and the pursuit of Happiness.

—United States Declaration of Independence

There still continues today . . . to be just an incredible array of negative stereotypes about native people. . . .We have in this country way too many negative stereotypes about black people, and about Latin people, and all kinds of people; it's just an incredible problem we deal with. . . . Everybody's sitting around this table, and they're all looking at each other with stereotypes, and they can't get past that. It's like everybody's sitting there and they have some kind of veil over their face, and they look at each other through this veil that makes them see each other through some stereotypical kind of viewpoint. If we're ever gonna collectively begin to grapple with the problems that we have collectively, we're gonna have to move back the veil and deal with each other on a more human level.

—Wilma Mankiller (1993), former
chief of the Cherokee Nation

Through our own efforts to create equity and excellence in our schools and through our research on equitable and excellent public schools and districts (e.g., Scheurich, 1998; Scheurich, Skrla, & Johnson, 2000; Skrla & Scheurich, 2001), we have come to understand the central importance of individual and shared beliefs. Some people call these beliefs or "values," some call them "ethics," others call them "commitments."

If you are going to successfully lead a school to attain both equity and excellence, you first have to believe it is possible. If you don't have that belief, you are going to have to develop it because having, deepening, and sustaining this belief is central to convincing others, central to maintaining this belief over the long haul, and central to creating equitable and excellent schools.

Take a few moments to think about your answer to the following reflective question: *Do I—deep inside where my most firmly held and private beliefs reside—truly believe it is possible in the immediate future to create and sustain schools in which literally all children will be highly successful?* Try to make a distinction for yourself between whether you *want* to believe that this is possible as some idealized dream, or whether you really believe that it *is* possible in the immediate present.

If you decide that your answer to this question is "yes," then the content of this chapter will be useful to you in sustaining and deepening that belief and in communicating it to others who may not share it. If you decide that your answer to the question—at this point—is that you *want* to believe that truly excellent and equitable schools are possible in the ideal, but that you do not really believe that such schools are achievable, then the discussion that follows hopefully will help you understand and change that belief.

First, we will discuss some barriers you may have that prevent you from believing in the reality of equitable and excellent schools. Second, we will discuss strategies for acquiring the belief if you don't already have it. Then, we will discuss what it means once you do have such a belief.

BARRIERS TO BELIEVING

Why do people, why do teachers and administrators, believe that children of color and/or children from low-income homes will, in general or on average, not do well in school? (When we use the phrases "on average" or "in general," we understand that there are always exceptions.) Certainly, it is true that, on average, children of color and children from low-income homes do not currently do as well in school as white middle-class children. This is a well-known fact, which is commonly referred to as the "achievement gap" in U.S. education. The important question, though, is why does this gap exist?

You probably have some answers to this in your mind. Most educators do, as do most other people. The most common answers educators and the general public give have to do with causes that are external to education, as Haycock (2001, p. 9-10) found in her research:

> Over the past five years, staff members at the Education Trust have shared . . . data on the achievement gap with hundreds of audiences all over the United States. During that time, we've learned a lot about what people think is going on.
>
> When we speak with adults, no matter where we are in the country, they make the same comments [about the children who are on the wrong side of the achievement gap]. "They're too poor." "Their parents don't care." "They come to school without an adequate breakfast." "They don't have enough books in the home." "Indeed, there aren't enough parents in the home." Their reasons, in other words, are always about the children and their families.

The typical external cause answers we most often hear are similar to those expressed by Education Trust's interviewees. These include that some children are genetically less intelligent, that some parents do not know how to help their children succeed in school, that the culture of the children and parents does not value or support education, and that the child does not come to school "ready to learn" with skills and attitudes needed to succeed.

Of course, anyone who has heard any one of these answers probably has heard several, as they are commonly circulated among educators and the general public. Many of these answers are interconnected or interrelated, but the point of all of them is that the cause or causes for the differences in achievement among different student groups is external to the educational system and, thus, not the fault or responsibility of educators. That is, if any of these or a combination of any or all of these external causes is the answer to why children of color, children from low-income families, and/or children of different cultures or home languages do not do as well in school, then, seemingly, we as educators are not at fault. This means the so-called achievement gap is not our responsibility.

It is very worrisome that the answer educators give results in the conclusion that educators have no responsibility for the achievement gap. It seems all too easy, even self-serving or self-protecting, for us to give an answer that relieves us of any responsibility. Perhaps we should be suspicious of such easy answers. Let's think about this.

First, the common belief in genetics as the cause of differences in educational achievement requires us to be very direct about what such a belief means. If someone believes in genetics as the reason children of color and children from low-income homes do not do as well in school as middle-class white children, it means that this person believes that people of color and people with low incomes are not as smart as white middle-class people and that the cause of this difference is genetic. This means that people of color and low income generally are genetically born with less intelligence than are white middle-class people. In fact, this is the argument made in a fairly recent, though controversial, book, *The Bell Curve* (Herrnstein & Murray, 1996).

Although we know from research done by some of our students that many more educators actually believe in this genetics explanation than is commonly thought (see Marx, 2002; McKenzie, 2002), it is really a deeply horrible and terribly wrong explanation. In fact, it unquestionably is blatant racism. The overwhelming, inarguable conclusion of thousands of scientists all over the world is that this belief is false (see the following books for a thorough debunking of *The Bell Curve* and its arguments: *Intelligence, Genes, and Success: Scientists Respond to* The Bell Curve, Devlin, Resnick, & Roeder, 1998; *The Bell Curve Wars: Race, Intelligence, and the Future of America*, Fraser, 1995; and *Measured Lies:* The Bell Curve *Examined*, Kincheloe, Steinberg, & Gresson, 1996). As science has progressed, especially as genetic science has progressed, it has repeatedly been shown that any belief that there is a genetic difference in intelligence by race or income is totally, unquestionably, inarguably false. It is very simple: We are all the same human beings. Appearance differences, such as skin color or the shape of one's eyes or the size of one's nose, are completely irrelevant to intelligence.

Yes, there are a few books, like *The Bell Curve*, and a few scientists that argue the opposite, but they represent only a tiny, tiny percentage of the scientific evidence relevant to this matter. To believe today in a genetic difference in intelligence for the different races is similar to believing that the earth is flat (in fact, scientists have concluded that trying to separate out different "races" is virtually impossible; race is not a fact, it is a social construction). The absurdity of such a belief is beyond question, but sadly, painfully, this belief does continue, even among educators.

Now, some people would say to us, "Why do you even legitimate this genetic explanation by discussing it?" The reason we discuss it is that in our experience, and in the work other researchers and our own students have done, there continues to be a significant number of educators who still believe in a genetic explanation—especially because there continue to be many who hold this as a hidden or covert belief. This means that they know it is politically incorrect to express this belief, but inside they continue to believe it—and this belief drives their actions as educators and as citizens.

We do not think it is useful to conceal the fact that this genetics-oriented racism still exists. In addition, even many who do not centrally hold this view have a little bit of it left in their minds. In fact, if we could be totally honest, all of us probably have a little bit of it in the corners of our consciousness and unconsciousness. The historical past just does not disappear overnight, and this genetic difference belief was once dominant—historically speaking, not very long ago— among virtually all white people in U.S. society. (For an excellent discussion of the history of this belief in the United States, see Valencia's 1997 book *The Evolution of Deficit Thinking* and, further, his 2000 book *Intelligence Testing and Minority Students*). Consequently, all of us must be very careful that this old belief may still hold some barely conscious or some unconscious influence on our thinking.

Most educators, though, have consciously left this belief behind. Instead, the answers that now dominate responses to the question of what is the external cause of children of color and children of low-income families not doing as well as others, in general, in our schools, are what might be called *social* answers. By social, we mean the cause is not seen as physical or genetic; it is seen as arising out of a social situation, context, or history.

These social causes are all those, besides the genetic one, that we offered earlier: (a) Some parents do not know how to help their children succeed in school; (b) the culture of the children and parents does not value or support education; or (c) the child does not come to school "ready to learn" with skills and attitudes needed to succeed in school.

All of these social causes seem like reasonable or acceptable explanations to most of us today. However, these are a complex set of causes. Some of them are factually true in some sense. For instance, middle-class white parents do typically know more than low-income parents or parents of color know about how to help their children succeed in school as school is typically conducted today (Delgado-Gaitan, 1992). Moreover, some children, including those from low-income homes and many children of color, begin school with fewer formal educational experiences than do other children who may have had the benefits of preschool. However, how these "facts" are true—in some ways, but not in other ways—is a complex issue, which we will address here as we go along.

In regard to the beliefs that educators hold about the external social causes of differences in achievement, research shows that many of these beliefs are factually false. For example, recent research (that has been undertaken in more culturally sensitive ways than was research conducted in the past) shows that members of cultural groups often labeled as "uncaring" about their children's education—that is, African Americans and Mexican Americans—strongly support the education of their children (see Delpit, 1996; Lopez, Scribner, & Mahitivanichcha, 2001). In other research done when one of us, as part of a research team, interviewed adults who had grown up as children in families that did migrant agricultural work, the research participants repeatedly said that all of the migrant parents they had known believed strongly in education (for some of these interviews, see *The Labors of Life/Labores de la Vida*, Guajardo, Sanchez, Fineman, & Scheurich, 1999, a documentary video available through the lead author of this book).

Nonetheless, we know that, in fact, many educators do not believe that parents of color or members of cultures of color want or care about educational success for their children. We know that many educators can come up with what they see as examples proving that these parents and their culture do not care. Yes, there are some parents of color who don't care about their children doing well in school, but there are also many white middle-class parents who don't care about their children not doing well in school. However, when researchers carefully and sensitively study parents of all races and cultures, they find that virtually all parents strongly want their children to be successful in school and will do whatever they can to support that success.

Unfortunately, some of the research that several of our doctoral students have done shows that many teachers harbor cultural, racial, and class stereotypes about parents of color and low-income parents (see Marx, 2002; McKenzie, 2002). This research shows that even when faced with factual evidence to the contrary, many teachers continue to hold fast to stereotypes, labeling the factual and research evidence as the exception and not the rule. For example, some who teach children of color have a strong belief that very few of their students' parents care about schooling. Even if contrary examples are pointed out, these teachers still cling to their belief, often by citing exceptions they know about. When these teachers were asked in McKenzie's research whether they knew the parents or had been to their homes, their answer was typically "no." After working with these teachers to get them to reflect on these beliefs, McKenzie concluded that the teachers strongly protected their negative stereotypes about the parents—in the face of evidence to the contrary—to justify their own lack of success with the children of color in their classrooms.

This presents us with a difficult problem. How many of us are so heavily invested in our stereotypes that we resist contradictory information? Indeed, isn't that how a stereotype works—by ignoring and resisting evidence to the contrary? Why do some of us strongly hold on to the belief that parents of color and low-income parents don't care? Why do some of us believe that cultures of color do not value education? Why are some of us working so hard to find an external justification for our lack of success with our children of color? What if it is our problem instead of our children's parents' problem?

Part of this stereotype against parents of color and their parenting is held because the white middle class (of which teachers, overwhelmingly, are a part) has a picture or characterization of correct parenting that differs from the approach to parenting in other cultures. For instance, the middle class tend to believe that children should be raised directly by the parents, whereas people in some cultural groups, including many Latino, Native American, and African American cultural groups, believe that grandparents or older uncles and aunts (some of whom may not even be blood relatives) can and should play major roles in raising children. Many white middle-class people then assume that any child not raised mainly by the parents is at a deficit as far as schooling is concerned. However, we know of no evidence that shows that children raised by extended family members do not do as well in school as children raised by their parents.

Another part of maintaining the stereotype is that "looking down" on some other group makes us feel better, makes us feel superior. Perhaps, even our identities as a people are wrapped up in having some groups to feel superior to. Besides, if these other groups are not inferior, then we may have to conclude that not being successful with children of color or children from low-income families is really mainly our fault, rather than theirs.

Educators, though, need to understand that these kinds of conclusions about parents and cultures of color cannot be supported by research, nor are they useful or productive if we are going to create equitable and excellent schools. It is extremely important that we recognize that we live in a multicultural society and that different cultures often do things in different ways. We also must recognize that children from many different cultures and cultural patterns of parenting can do well in school.

Furthermore, we need to recognize that we can create schools that value, appreciate, honor, and incorporate other cultures, and we don't mean just through food and holidays. We mean through deep connection and engagement with all of the parents and cultures of our children. As some (e.g., Ladson-Billings, 1994; Moll, 1992) have suggested, educators in typical schools often assume unconsciously that the values, beliefs, behaviors, and other attributes of the white middle class are the right and best ones, even when the schools that these educators work in serve children solely from other cultures. However, too many people who daily practice and love their own cultures have become successful in business, scholarship, sciences, the arts, and other fields for us to assume that the white middle-class culture is the only right way to do anything. Yes, as Delpit (1996) and others have suggested, children of color need to learn the white middle-class culture because it is so pervasive, but this doesn't mean that we cannot also learn and value deeply all cultures within our country. Indeed, the main culture of this country, the white middle-class one, has always been a deep intermixture of numerous other cultures. Thus, the idea that the culture of one group has to be the only one used in schooling is really silly.

Our job as educators, then, is twofold. First, we need to confront our own beliefs about parents and cultures of color. Second, and also very important, we ought to engage with these parents and cultures in a positive way (in particular, see the work of Moll, 1992, and Gonzalez, Moll, & Tenery, 1995, for an assets orientation to other cultures; see also Kuykendall's *From Rage to Hope*, 1992). Rather than trying to find deficits or negatives that we can posit as causes for the achievement gap, we need to understand and focus on the assets in these cultures so that we can build positively on them to educate all the children of our country's different cultures.

We have, however, still left one area unaddressed. This is the assumption that parents of color and low-income parents do not understand what they need to be doing with their children to prepare them for school, or that these parents do not themselves have the school skills to pass along to their children, or both. The result of either or both of these factors is that children of color and children of low-income parents do not have the attitudes, skills, and/or knowledge that we commonly believe children need to come to school with to do well in school or, at least, to start school properly prepared. The head-line of a recent editorial in *Education Week* (Price, 2001, p. 48) addressed this issue in the following way: "The Preparation Gap: Eliminate It First, Then the Achievement Gap."

While this may seem like a simple issue, it is, like other issues we have discussed here, actually more complex than is commonly assumed. It is a fact that, on average, white middle-class children do start school with more school success atti-tudes, skills, and knowledge than do children of color and children from low-income families—given the way school is currently conducted.

For the moment, let's give those of us who believe in this external cause the benefit of the doubt. Let's say there is a "preparation gap" that precedes the "achievement gap," as the *Education Week* editorialist wrote. Let's, just for a moment, say that, on average, parents of color and low-income parents don't prepare their children for success in school in ways that are a good match for the schools their children will attend.

Even if this is taken to be true, does this mean we cannot be educationally successful with these children? Is it an inarguable inevitability that if parents don't properly prepare their children in advance of sending them to school, there is no way we can succeed educationally with their children? For example, do educators want to say that if some children are not prepared to begin reading instruction in kindergarten, there is virtually no way we can get these children to grade level on reading skills? This is what we are saying when we argue that the reason we have an achievement gap is because children are not properly prepared by their parents for school success. We are committing to the algorithm that if A (proper preparation by parents) is not there, then we cannot teach our students so that they will achieve B (school success).

If we think about it this way, the algorithm is false; it is just not true. We, in fact, have multiple programs, curricula, and methodologies for teaching children to read, do math, and write. No matter how "unprepared" a child comes to school, we already have many methods, curricula, and programs that have been shown to be successful with unprepared children. You only have to read, for example, *Education Week*, *Phi Delta Kappan*, or *Educational Leadership* for one year, and you will see articles about all kinds of approaches educators have devised that are successful with children who have not come to school prepared for school. Also, there are already many classrooms and schools, just like those we all work within, that are highly successful with these so-called unprepared children.

If many teachers and administrators already know how to achieve success with unprepared children, then anyone who wants to develop an equitable and excellent classroom or school can learn to do the same. The easiest thing, the thing that many educators do when they personally do not know how to accomplish success with the unprepared child is to automatically blame the external cause and then do nothing to find out how they might change what they do or how they might learn something new that will help their students succeed. Thus, those who stop and say they can't are creating and living a dead end for themselves—and for their children.

This is the real problem in our view. Many of us want to be successful with all children without learning anything new. The issue is not really that it cannot be done. We know more than enough, as Ron Edmonds (1979) used to say, to educate any child well. The real point is whether we have the will to educate any child—whether we are willing to change, to learn new skills, new programs, new assumptions, new attitudes.

Thus, even if we grant that, on average, some groups of children do come to school not prepared in expected ways, it is *not* true that we do not have any means to be successful with them if that is what we are really committed to accomplish.

OK, now we have gotten to the point of suggesting that even if we accept that some children come without the same preparation other children come with, we can still be successful with any child. If this is true, then we should, we think, dump the whole concept of "unprepared." It is a deficit idea; it starts us off with a negative attitude toward children, as if they are missing something, lacking something, have less, are less. We think that virtually everyone would agree that if you want to be successful with teaching anything to any student, it is not useful to start with a deficit view of any student who needs to learn something.

In the place of this deficit view, we would suggest, as others have, an assets-oriented view toward all students. For all children, rather than starting out with a focus on what some child or some group of children do not have—like home preparation to learn reading in English—let's start with an assets-oriented view of each child and every group of children. Let's start with asking the question "What assets does this child or this group of children bring to school with them that we can use positively to build on to be educationally successful with this child or this group of children?" Isn't this how we ourselves would best like to be treated? Don't we want others to assume we have assets, strengths, that we can use to build upon in learning something new?

This is not really a revolutionary idea. Let's say you want to build a house. You used to live where wood was abundant and cheap so most houses were built out of wood. However, now you live where wood is scarce and expensive, but rock is abundant and cheap. Do you now say that you can't build a house because wood is too hard to get and more expensive than you can afford?

You don't say this if you really want a house, but that is the equivalent of what we in education often say. We are so used to wood houses (i.e., used to creating schools that are academically successful with only white middle-class children), we say we can't learn to build rock houses (i.e., learn to educate children from other, different social groups or cultures). However, it always makes much more sense to build with what is available. This is what an assets-oriented view means. You positively build with and on the assets that already exist, on what is already available. If wood is your asset, build with wood; if rock is your asset, build with rock. If an African American culture, a Mexican American culture, a working-class culture, an extended family, or a language other than English are the assets available, build positively on and with these assets.

For example, if a student's culture provides stronger support for group learning than individual learning, let's use that positively as an asset. This does not mean we don't sometimes use individual learning, but we start by building positively on the assets the children bring to school with them: the cultural assets, the home and family assets, and so on. Or, let's say that within a student's home context, older children are routinely expected to provide care for younger children. Let's use this as an asset in education. Let's have the older children assist in teaching the younger children.

Often migrant children are seen as being at a deficit, but research on their lives indicates they often hold more responsibility in the family than middle-class children hold in theirs, that they often have seen more of the "world" than their peers have, and that they have had to work much harder than most middle-class white children ever will. In fact, don't we often value those who understand how to do really hard work? Don't some even berate middle-class families for not teaching their children to work hard? If you want people who understand hard work, you want migrant workers and their children. Thus, let's look for and view experiences of different cultures and different ways of life as a positive, as assets to build education on.

Indeed, in a research project that one of us was involved with, led by our colleagues Pedro Reyes, Lonnie Wagstaff, and Jay Scribner (see Reyes, Scribner, & Paredes Scribner, 1999), it was found that in some schools and districts migrant children typically did as well as any other students and in some cases routinely did better. Why? The answer is because these successful schools and districts did not characterize these students as being in or having a deficit. Instead, these schools and districts were perceptive about the lives of these students, highly valued these students, built positively on their assets, and created programs, methods, procedures, and ways to ensure that they too could be academically successful. In short, there was nothing wrong with the students or their lives (i.e., deficit thinking), and no one treated the students as if there were. The problem is how we characterize the lives of our children, how we value them and their cultures, how we see the assets in their lives, and how we build positively on those assets.

As we mentioned before, this is the very point that scholars like Ladson-Billings (1994) or Moll (1992) have made. Ladson-Billings and others, like Hollins (1994), recommend that we positively use the culture that the child brings to school to successfully educate that child. Moll takes his preservice teachers out to the communities in which their children live so the teachers will learn the assets of those communities and so they can use those assets positively in their classrooms and schools. Moll says that all children have "funds of knowledge" that come from their experiences, their families, their communities, and their cultures and that we should use those assets, those funds of knowledge, in positive ways to successfully educate children. We believe that this idea or this approach, whether it is called "assets-based," "culturally congruent pedagogy," or "funds of knowledge," is a powerful idea that we should all learn to use.

Our job as educators is to be educators of all children. To be an educator is to be an expert at successfully teaching children—any and all children, not just some children. We would question whether we can legitimately call ourselves educational professionals if we can only successfully teach children from one group (like white middle-class children, for instance), or if we can only teach the way we were taught when we were children, or if we are restricted to being successful with only those children who fit the way we were taught to teach in college five, ten, or fifteen years ago. An educational professional, in our view, is one who can accomplish his or her work given new situations, new students, or new contexts. If we only know how to serve one kind of child and insist that we cannot succeed with any other kind of child, we simply do not understand how we can claim that teaching is a real profession or that educators are real professionals.

Our job as educators is to be professional experts at teaching children—no matter who those children are, where they come from, or what they bring with them or do not bring with them. If we don't know how to be successful with some particular child or some group of children, our professional commitment and our professional expertise should drive us to find out how others are doing what we do not yet know or, if necessary, to create new solutions.

As we said in the first chapter, we think we can be smarter and more creative than just continuing to use the old methods that don't work for diverse children. In every field of human endeavor, people have faced new situations of all sorts and have found solutions. In every field, there have come times when many said we couldn't; then some said they could, and they did. Actually, we don't think it is really that difficult to successfully teach *all* children if we just decide that we can.

In fact, there are already available many different solutions that educators have already devised to successfully educate all students. If we will just get rid of the "can't," decide that we can, and start looking around for those answers, we will find them. Teachers and whole schools are already succeeding educationally with any child in any context that we have or can imagine. We only have to explore, read, and work at it to find these teachers and schools. We can learn to educate differently. We can learn to educate all of the children that are in our classrooms and our schools. Really, the most important barrier is in our minds, in our beliefs—not in some external cause.

LEARNING TO BELIEVE

The best way to acquire a belief in the possibility that literally all children can be highly successful in school is to experience for yourself schools where this is the case. Many teachers and school leaders of color and those from low-income homes do not have to become convinced that all children can succeed because they themselves were those children. They know firsthand from their own experience that "all children can learn." Other educators work in schools in which excellence and equity are realities, and they have learned directly from their coworkers and colleagues how to teach and administer in ways that create such success. For example, one of us had a white woman student who as a new reading teacher started in an urban school dominated by children of color from low-income families. She had all the barriers we talked about above, and she definitely had a deficit attitude about the children in her classroom. However, she was lucky enough to go to a school in which there was a strong group of Latina teachers who themselves had come out of low-income Mexican American families. They worked with her and mentored her so that she changed her beliefs, and, as a result, she became highly successful with her diverse children. Then, when we asked her whether it was possible to get children of color from low-income homes to read on grade level even if they had not been prepared to read by their parents, her answer was "of course." What had she learned that the rest of us need to learn?

If you have not had such success experiences yourself, one excellent way to develop a belief in equity and excellence is to go see classrooms, schools, and districts that are accomplishing such success or are making great strides toward accomplishing it. Another way is to talk to others who have chosen the same journey of equity and excellence. Some of these educators will have come to believe in the journey, and some will be on their way toward believing it—just as you are—and they will be from all races and cultures. Wherever anyone is on this journey, they will have good information, ideas, or experiences to share. So, in your school, your district, your city, nearby areas, your state, or at conferences, seek out others who are on this same journey. Seek out those who are already achieving equity and excellence and those who are learning to do so. Become friends with these people and share with and support each other. Build a network of those committed to gaining equity and excellence in our nation's schools.

Another thing that will help you to believe in equity and excellence is to read about it. This book will help you. There are also many articles and books that can be found through libraries and the Internet and through professional organizations, like the Association for Supervision and Curriculum Development (ASCD). Indeed, ASCD constantly presents workshops and conference sessions on this subject and publishes many books and videos on it. It is a treasure trove for this kind of material, but it is only one among many others, including the publisher of this book.

Finally, some people can just make a leap of faith. These people say to themselves, "Equity and excellence are the right things to believe in. I may not know now how to do it, but I am going to make a leap of faith that I can do it. Somehow I will figure it out, and I will not quit until I do."

CONCLUSION

Let's say we are now in this place together. We are now on the same train. We believe that it is possible to develop schools that are both equitable and excellent. We have visited other classrooms and schools that have already become both equitable and excellent. We have connected with and developed relationships with others with the same commitments. We have read about it. We have disposed of or are working hard to dispose of any barriers we might have had at some point to achieving such success. We no longer believe that external causes are sufficient reasons to not educate all children well. We have switched from a deficits orientation to an assets orientation in our thinking about all children. We no longer focus on what children don't have; we now focus instead on what assets they do have and how we might build on those assets so that all children can be educationally successful.

Thus, we have decided that our job, our work, our commitment as educators or as educational leaders is to develop classrooms and schools that are both equitable and excellent. We believe in it. We are going to do it! But what now, where do we go next? That is what the rest of this book is about. The rest of this book covers specific areas related to helping you "do it." However, before we go there, let's pause a moment.

To create an equitable and excellent classroom or school, we need to make the commitment to do this the heart of our efforts. Every day, every week, we need to reaffirm our commitment to this. This is a righteous journey, a democratic journey, a spiritual journey. However, it is not always going to be easy. Sometimes, we all will get down or depressed. There will be failures; there will be barriers and difficulties. There will be some who will work hard to stand in our way or make fun of us, who will call us naive or idealistic. However, those who succeed at any great endeavor—and this is a great endeavor—do not allow excuses, do not allow themselves to stay stuck in "down" or "failures" or "difficulties." Those who succeed say to themselves that no matter what, "I am—we are—going to succeed!" They just won't quit; they just will not take any excuses. Moreover, even if we have not done this in the past, any of us can start now. We can decide that we are going to be the ones who carry this great endeavor forward.

This is simply too important for us to fail or quit at. This *is* a great endeavor. We are on the front lines of a great and truly important civil rights struggle. We are the carriers, the foot soldiers, of a mighty dream of equity in this country. Every day in our classrooms and schools, we are either moving this dream forward or we are not. Its success is in our hands, individually and collectively. Remember, we didn't choose money, or fame, or power; we chose to be teachers. We chose to be able to say that when our work is done, its effects aren't just big houses or fancy cars. We don't strive to see our names in the news all the time. What we do as teachers and school leaders, even if society will not adequately reward our work or recognize it, is the very foundation of the future of our society. We teachers and leaders are the ones who make this future. If it is to be an equitable one, if we are to realize the dream, it really is in our hands. We are the ones who can make the dream come true.

In the next chapter we address the large issue of standards and curriculum, an issue that is currently receiving considerable public and educator attention. We discuss why we think standards and curriculum alignment are necessities for equitable and excellent schooling.

CHAPTER THREE

Standards and Curriculum

> *I believe that the community's duty to education is, therefore, its paramount moral duty. By law and punishment, by social agitation and discussion, society can regulate and form itself in a more or less haphazard and chance way. But through education society can formulate its own purposes, can organize its own means and resources, and thus shape itself with definiteness and economy in the direction in which it wishes to move.*
>
> —John Dewey (1897), pioneer U.S. educator

WHY USE STANDARDS?

State or national school curriculum standards are a contested and sometimes controversial topic. Such standards elicit both strong support and heated opposition from educators and others. However, with the passage of the *No Child Left Behind Act of 2001* (for full information about the act, go to www.nochildleftbehind.gov), the central importance of standards has grown considerably, as has accountability. Our focus, though, is whether standards, at the school, district, and/or state levels, can be positively used in the work of creating equitable and excellent schools. Our conclusion is that standards are one of the keys in accomplishing this work. (There will be some coverage of accountability policy systems and accountability tests in this chapter because they are closely related to standards, but most of our coverage of accountability will occur in Chapter 6.)

The reason we support standards is that, historically, when educational systems in this country have been left fairly open, loosely defined, and unmonitored as to what is taught, when, and to whom—that is, when there have been no standards—children of color and children from low-income families have suffered. This is because the less clearly defined and detailed the rules or criteria for success are in a system, the more the system tends to favor the already privileged or advantaged individuals within the system (Bourdieu, 1982). In contrast, for every child to have a good and positive chance at success, it is very important that the criteria for success (proficiency in reading, writing, mathematics, science, history, the arts, etc.) be spelled out in advance, clearly and specifically, so that everyone (children, parents, teachers, administrators, and community members) can understand what the criteria are. This is what high quality standards can do, when carefully and consistently applied.

Based on our research (e.g., Skrla, Scheurich, & Johnson, 2000), and that of others (e.g., Capper, Keyes, & Frattura, 2000; Cawelti, 1999; Cohen & Hill, 2001; Edmonds, 1986; Reyes, Scribner, & Paredes Scribner, 1999), it is clear that schools and districts that are highly successful with all students *always* have clear, consistent curriculum standards that are known and used by all teachers. For instance, one of the very first steps that Aldine Independent School District—a sizeable, diverse, urban school district in Texas—took in starting their impressive year-to-year improvement of achievement by children of color and children from low-income families was to align their entire curriculum with state standards and with state assessment targets (see Koschoreck, 2001; Skrla et al., 2000).

In some cases, the standards in use in schools come from the work of national professional organizations, such as the

National Council of Teachers of English (NCTE) or the National Council of Teachers of Mathematics (NCTM). In other cases, the standards are specified by the state in which the school is located. In still other cases, standards have been developed by local curriculum committees. Perhaps most commonly, the standards in use incorporate and draw on all of these sources. For example, most mathematics standards at all levels have been strongly influenced by the work of NCTM in this regard. However, in all cases, the teachers and administrators use the standards to set target goals for what all children should know and be able to do in each subject at each grade level.

We cannot overstate the importance of this point. Our research, as well as that of others, has shown that clear curriculum standards are virtually a necessity for equitable and excellent schools. The idea is to create a whole educational system in which all educators explicitly know specifically what they need to accomplish to be successful with all their students. Ronald Edmonds (1986), the father of the effective schools movement and one of our heroes, emphasized this same reliance on standards in describing the schools he studied:

> The teachers in the effective schools . . . make it clear that they are working with a minimum academic prerequisite and that they expect everybody to achieve it. They may expect variability in pupil performance, but they do not expect than any significant number of children of any race or social class will fail to demonstrate minimum mastery. (p. 99)

While contemporary standards have typically risen above "minimum mastery," in the successful schools and districts that we have studied, clear standards for mastery of academic content played an important role in the schools' ability to be highly successful with all students.

In addition, it is our judgment that standards are here to stay. There is just too much broad public support for them both inside and outside of education for us to think that they are going to go away anytime soon. Our approach is that rather than complaining about standards because they impose too much rigidity on schooling or because they limit teachers, teaching, and the curriculum, we should figure out how to appropriate the standards to our mission to serve all children well and learn how to use the standards appropriately in a positive way, as teachers and administrators in successful schools have done. However, as with all we do in education, we ought to support continuing critique of the standards because there is always considerable room for improvement and because, in general, critique tends to cause us to rethink, reconsider, and improve. In addition, we all need to understand that we are on a trajectory with working with standards and that, if we persist in this focus, the quality will improve, as it already has in many states (see Linn, Baker, & Betebenner, 2002).

There are, of course, significant challenges to be faced in learning to use standards in the service of excellent and equitable schools. One of the main challenges is the variability of the quality and utility in current state standards. Some states have standards that have been judged to be excellent, some adequate, and some poor. Information about state standards, including databases and ratings, can be found on Web sites maintained by Achieve, Inc. (www.achieve.org), the American Federation of Teachers (www.aft.org), Mid-continent Research for Education and Learning (www.mcrel.org), and *Education Week* (www.edweek.org). Our advice is to find out the quality of your school's, district's, or state's standards, and, if they are weak, to supplement them with those from other sources. This should not be ignored, because it is just too easy today to get both district and state standards on the Web and to get quality judgments of the main standards sets, mostly on the Web also.

A related issue is the fact that, according to the most recent research (see, e.g., American Federation of Teachers, 2001), virtually no state has its standards and accountability procedures, including its state assessments, closely matched. (Although most people talk about the "alignment" of standards and accountability tests, we will use the terms *matched* or *correlated* when discussing this relationship so as not to confuse this discussion with one about the alignment of the curriculum.) This means that the specific areas that a state's standards cover for a particular subject or grade do not necessarily closely match, or correlate with, the specific areas that the state's accountability tests cover for a particular subject or grade. While this lack of match or correlation seems illogical, it is a current fact. States have simply not done a sufficiently good job at making sure that their accountability tests are a good, thorough, and comprehensive testing of what is set out in their standards. However, some states, like Texas, are in the second generation of their efforts to produce matched standards and, thus, have made significant improvements.

Elsewhere, however, this lack of a close match between standards and accountability tests creates problems, but they are solvable ones. They are not, however, small problems or ones that you can ignore. For example, if you just follow your state's standards without simultaneously checking what areas the accountability tests cover, you can get caught with your students not knowing some key area when they take your state's accountability tests. So, again, be sure that your school or district is paying close attention to coverage in each subject or grade of both standards *and* accountability tests.

Another problem that has been raised with standards is that they may have a cultural bias that puts some students at a disadvantage (Fox, 2001). We would agree that standards are culturally biased. In fact, we would suggest that it is impossible for humans to produce any social product that is not culturally biased. If we could have whatever we wanted, we would have the standards be deeply multicultural because that is what this country has always been since its very beginnings, and it is even more so today. As this critique and others demonstrate, it is always true that we should critique standards and be working on constantly improving them.

However, in the interim, while standards are not multicultural, we would advise using the point that Delpit (1996) has made. All children need to learn the ways of the dominant culture, the white middle-class culture, which standards to date largely reflect. This does not mean, though, that we cannot value the other cultures that our children bring with them, nor does it mean that we cannot use these various cultures positively in teaching the standards we currently have. We think the teachers that Ladson-Billings (1994) portrays in *The Dreamkeepers* would have little trouble valuing the home culture of their children while teaching the standards required by the state. We also think that teachers who understand Delpit's work would want to teach their children both the dominant culture and their children's own.

THE NECESSITY OF CURRICULUM ALIGNMENT

In order for everyone at all levels within a school or school district to have a clear understanding of what the curriculum standards are for each subject area at each grade level, and in order for teachers to teach all of the content specified by the standards for each subject and grade, curriculum alignment is an absolute necessity (English & Steffy, 2001). Many schools and districts are already engaged in this work or have made initial attempts to align standards with what is taught and tested.

Nonetheless, curriculum alignment is a large, time- and effort-intensive undertaking. Given the limitations of any particular context, larger districts or a collaboration of a group of several smaller districts may be better equipped to work through the alignment process, but the work can be accomplished by any committed, dedicated school staff. If you are in a school in which the district is not supportive of a larger curriculum alignment effort, we would suggest that you find a district that has already undertaken such an effort and see if you can get them to share their work with you and your school. Our experience has been that the best districts are already aligning their curriculum and that they are willing to share their work with those in a district in which there is not district support for this kind of work. Some districts even have their materials posted on district Web sites (see, e.g., those of the Aldine Independent School District at www.aldine.k12.tx.us/parents/curriculum.htm).

One highly important part of accomplishing this curriculum alignment is that teachers and administrators who are highly respected in the district or districts undertaking this work be centrally involved. In fact, in our view, it is almost a necessity that the teachers in the district respect the standards if they are actually going to be used well. As a result, those involved in the alignment should be highly respected by the teachers. Virtually everyone knows who these highly respected teachers are in each school and district, and they are the ones whose efforts really should be called on to accomplish this alignment. In addition, this undertaking must be continuous, year to year. As our research has shown (Scheurich et al., 2000), state standards and accountability systems frequently change, sometimes yearly. Thus, rechecking the curriculum alignment for each grade and subject needs to be done annually.

How Alignment of Standards and Curriculum Works in Creating Equitable and Excellent Schools

To promote understanding of how aligning standards and curriculum can be an important and powerful part of your work to create a school in which all children are highly successful, we offer the following illustration. Get a copy of your state standards for the courses and grades in your school. Most states now have them in a downloadable fashion on a state-sponsored Web site. Alternatively, they are available through national databases such as those mentioned earlier in the chapter. For example, to examine the Texas standards, go to www.tea.state.tx.us. Find "Curriculum and Assessment" at the top right of this Web page. Just underneath this, click on

Figure 3.1   Example: Texas Mathematics Standards for Grade 1

1.1   Number, operation, and quantitative reasoning. The student uses whole numbers to describe and compare quantities. The student is expected to:

(a)   compare and order whole numbers up to 99 (less than, greater than, or equal to) using sets of concrete objects and pictorial models;

(b)   create sets of tens and ones using concrete objects to describe, compare, and order whole numbers;

(c)   use words and numbers to describe the values of individual coins such as penny, nickel, dime, and quarter and their relationships; and

(d)   read and write numbers to 99 to describe sets of concrete objects.

SOURCE: Texas Education Agency (1997).

TEKS, which are the "Texas Essential Knowledge and Skills," the standards for K-12 public education in Texas. On this new link, you can pick out which standards you want to see or download.

Let's say you are interested in mathematics standards. Click on Chapter 111, Mathematics. You can see on this Web page that the standards are divided by elementary, middle, and high school. Let's say, for instance, that you want to see the first-grade math standards. Click on the button to the left of "Mathematics Grade 1." You will then see the outline, or frame, for a mathematics standard for the first grade.

One section of these Texas first grade mathematics standards is displayed in Figure 3.1. Each school's job, then, is to ensure that all first-grade students learn these skills and acquire this knowledge.

The California standards for Grade 1 mathematics in this area are similar to that in the Texas illustration (see Figure 3.2). Other states have standards that are arranged in grade spans

Figure 3.2   Example: California Mathematics Standard for Grade 1

Number Sense

1.0   Students understand and use numbers up to 100.

1.1   Count, read, and write whole numbers to 100.

1.2   Compare and order whole numbers to 100 by using the symbols for less than, equal to, or greater than (<, =, >).

1.3   Represent equivalent forms of the same number through the use of physical models, diagrams, and number expressions (to 20) (e.g., 8 may be represented as $4 + 4, 5 + 3, 2 + 2 + 2 + 2, 10 - 2, 11 - 3$).

1.4   Count and group object in ones and tens (e.g., three groups of 10 and 4 equals 34, or $30 + 4$).

1.5   Identify and know the value of coins and show different combinations of coins that equal the same value.

SOURCE: California Department of Education (n.d.).

(e.g., K-4 mathematics) or different configurations of content areas.

Let's think through, then, what is involved. You need to have a curriculum for each grade and subject. This curriculum needs to incorporate standards that designate everything that is supposed to be taught or learned in any specific curriculum area, like third-grade math for instance. The problem in the past, though, has been that in many schools, the curriculum for a particular area either has been very loosely described or has been determined by the textbooks that the district or state has chosen. Those days are, thankfully, largely gone. The fact that we ever tried to run a public educational system without laying out what every student needed to learn in each content area and each year seems counterproductive and naive now.

We can understand, though, that those older ways gave teachers permission to teach whatever they wanted within some reasonable range. We can also understand that this teacher discretion was valuable for some teachers and some students, but this approach did not serve *all* students well. In fact, for those children whom schools did not traditionally serve well, there was almost no real curriculum and certainly no systematic and comprehensive curriculum. This was particularly true in schools dominated by children of color from low-income families. There were frequently no standards, and often no one seemed to care that this was true. It was often just assumed that these students would fail and that there was nothing anyone could do about this.

We ran into a good example of this in our own research. We have frequently mentioned the Aldine, Texas, district, which has made such strong strides in improving the achievement of its students, who are predominantly children of color from low-income families. Before accountability and standards came to Texas in a strong way, the Aldine superintendent, Sonny Donaldson, thought the children of color in his district were doing well because each year one of them got into a service academy, like West Point, or went to an Ivy League school. However, when accountability and standards did come in, he quickly found out that the children of color were doing so poorly in math and reading that there were virtually no standards in his district for these children.

Unfortunately, this was typical of many places. For children of color and children from low-income homes, there simply were no standards. There was no closely defined curriculum that teachers had to cover, let alone succeed with, and no accountability for student learning. While this "freedom" benefited a few teachers and kids, mostly it left the least privileged children with the least learning.

In our view, however, standards do not really need to significantly limit any teachers or teaching, or narrow the curriculum. Standards simply designate all that needs to be learned in a given course, grade, or subject area. Good teachers would certainly want to teach all those areas whether standards existed or not. In addition, standards need not hinder the creativity of teachers in their teaching methods. The creativity or excellence of a teacher is not so much about the content of what is being taught, but about the way it is being taught. For example, if to teach math a good teacher builds on the culture or lived context of his or her children, this same approach can be used no matter what needs to be covered in the standards. In addition, those teachers teaching the most advanced children can certainly exceed the standards.

Another significant problem that standards addressed, besides the one of virtually no standards for children of color and children from low-income families, is that in the past, many schools and districts had never aligned their curricula. Without an aligned curriculum, the third-grade teacher has no clear idea of what subject area knowledge and skills the second-grade students were supposed to have been taught. Nor would this teacher have a clear idea of what she or he was supposed to teach so that the right foundation was created for the fourth-grade teacher. The following quote from an elementary teacher in an exemplary school serving a school population that consisted of a majority of children of color illustrates this point:

> I feel like [the district's instructional framework] is like a road map. In 1976 when I came to the district, straight out of college, there wasn't a road map for a new teacher. You came in the classroom, and you had a classroom, and you had some books on the shelf that you had to teach. And, yes, you had your curriculum guides. But you just didn't necessarily have a road map. The [district framework] is going to walk you through everything that you need to do. And it doesn't just carry over in [the state's accountability tests]. It carries over in your spelling, your reading. It's a road map that is going to help new and not so new

instructors in our district to go where we need to go and be successful.

In fact, it seems crazy that we had educational systems in which educators had no clear and specific idea about their place in the curriculum of a school or district. It simply does not work, when trying to serve all children equally well, to have a sequence of courses with no teacher knowing specifically what she or he has to get students to learn so that the entire sequence works. While there are certainly other ways to arrive at this alignment, it is simply a fact that it has largely been standards and accountability systems that have gotten a large percentage of schools and districts to address this lack of curriculum alignment, and that is a very valuable accomplishment.

Consequently, what is needed is for a school, a district, or, better, a state to specify the expected curriculum standards for all subjects and all grades. Then, all teachers could know specifically what their students are expected to have learned, in terms of knowledge and skills, before entering a particular class, and what the students need to learn before they can pass on to the next teacher and class.

Again, however, please remember that this curriculum and the alignment need to be correlated with not only a state's standards but also the state's accountability system. For example, if a fourth-grade accountability test will cover a particular writing skill, you must make sure that you will have covered that skill in your curriculum prior to the students taking the test, even if the skill is not listed as a standard by the state for that grade and subject. Again, don't be fooled; this lack of correlation between standards and testing happens very frequently, rather than rarely. Nonetheless, we do not make this point to get you to teach to the test, a practice that we discuss and totally condemn in Chapter 6. Our point is a warning that you cannot count on accountability tests covering only what is in the standards, and, thus, you do not want to leave your children vulnerable to failing on the tests because of what you have not yet taught them.

Also, please remember that what we are striving for here are equitable and excellent schools. This means, as we said, that we must have high quality standards, that virtually all students must meet them (excellence), and that there must be no difference in success among different groups of children by race, ethnicity, culture, income, or home language (equity). That is to say that in an equitable and excellent school, African American students meet the same high standards that middle-class white students meet. To accomplish this excellence, then, for all student groups and for all students, every teacher needs to know what he or she can expect from students entering his or her class at the beginning of the school year and what these students will be expected to know before they can enter the next class in the sequence. Thus, we would suggest that a school that does not have these two elements—standards and alignment—cannot become an equitable and excellent school. First, the school must have a schoolwide curriculum schema (standards) in all subjects and grades. Second, in an equitable and excellent school, *all* teachers must have a strong sense of the whole schema and a strong sense of their specific role in that schema.

There are state and national experts, consultants, who can help align a curriculum and help prepare teachers for an aligned curriculum. Furthermore, many states provide state-paid experts to help you do this. Sometimes you can hire someone from another district or school to assist you. Some educator organizations have experts available for your use. Whatever you do, please make sure you do it in a way that teachers will understand, believe in, support, and, above all, use. In other words, do not just have the curriculum aligned for you; involve your most respected educators with the internal or external experts you may be using. It certainly costs more and takes more personnel time to do this, but the payoff in teacher support and commitment to the curriculum (standards) is well worth the cost in time and money.

However, we want to take this one step further because the schools and districts we have studied have done so. The approach used by most of the schools and districts that have been highly successful with children of color and children from low-income families is to do more than just have curriculum standards that all teachers know. These successful schools and districts plan what areas of the curriculum will be covered at what time, typically weekly or even daily (this is what some call developing a "curriculum map"; for an example of what such a plan looks like, go to www.aldine.k12.tx.us/parents/curriculum/benchmarks/MATHfirst.pdf).

The reason schools and districts do this is not to control teachers. The reason they do this is, as we will discuss later, so that they will have teachers working together, working collaboratively, to improve their success as teachers. Thus, if teachers are teaching the same things at approximately the same time, they can collaborate on how they *all* can be successful with *all* of their students. These successful schools and districts, then, lay out a whole semester or a whole year of curriculum in every subject in every grade, and this includes what week each specific part of the curriculum will be taught.

Our purpose here, though, is not to explain how to do all of this. There are plenty of books and experts that you can use. Our purpose is to communicate the research-based importance of having standards, of having a curriculum that parallels those standards, of correlating or matching your curriculum with both your state's standards and its accountability system, and of having an aligned curriculum in which all teachers know their place in the curriculum system.

Conclusion

Before we turn, though, to instruction and classroom climate in the next chapter, we want to tell a brief story about two urban districts within the same state. The first district has just this past summer, the summer of 2002, created an aligned curriculum. They have struggled for years with facilitating academic success for their children of color and children from low-income homes. Ten years ago, in the second district, after the district leadership had decided that they were failing their children and that they wanted to do something about that fact, the superintendent turned to his deputy for advice on where to start. Her decision was to bring in, during the subsequent summer, the most respected teachers from throughout the district to benchmark and align the curriculum. The district did this, though the deputy conceded that there were lots of tears, conflicts, and struggle. Nonetheless, the work got done. The deputy also said that this effort was a major key in beginning the tremendous improvement that the district has seen over the past ten years in the academic achievement of its diverse children.

Of course, this benchmarking of the curriculum did not guarantee the second district the success that they have had over the past ten years. Nor does the fact that the leadership in the first district did not set standards or curriculum benchmarks and did not align their curriculum earlier *solely* account for their lack of success. However, from everything we have learned over the past ten years about schools and districts that are successful with literally all students, it is evident that the development of quality standards and the alignment of the curriculum are a necessity for significantly raising the achievement of children of color and children from low-income families. By taking these steps ten years ago, the second district laid the foundation for their subsequent success; by not doing so ten years ago, the first district substantially hindered their possibilities of creating the same kind of success, even though they serve highly similar student populations.

In the next chapter, we provide discussions of instruction and classroom climate that we believe will be helpful in the creation of equitable and excellent schooling. In particular, we will focus on high expectations and respect, culturally responsive teaching, loving and caring in the classroom, democratic and collaborative teaching environments, continuous development of content expertise, and discipline problems.

CHAPTER FOUR

Instruction and Classroom Climate

> *Our hope lies in schools that are more personal, compelling, and attractive than the Internet or TV, where youngsters can keep company with interesting and powerful adults, who are in turn in alliance with the students' families and local institutions. We need to surround kids with adults who know and care for our children, who have opinions and are accustomed to expressing them publicly, and who know how to reach reasonable collective decisions in the face of disagreement.*
>
> —Deborah Meier (2000), former principal of Central Park East School

What goes on in classrooms "to surround kids with adults who know and care for our children"? Classrooms that have high levels of achievement and serve diverse groups of learners are strikingly different from typical classrooms that fail to ably serve children of color and children from low-income homes. We know this from research that has accumulated over the past 25 years, beginning with and building upon the pioneering work of Edmonds (1979, 1986), among others.

Knowing that classroom practice that serves all children well exists is one thing; implementing it in thousands of classrooms across the United States and sustaining it through time is a different type of challenge altogether, as Ferguson (1998) emphasized in his work on closing achievement gaps:

> Credible claims of remarkable progress for a few students, a few classrooms, or a few schools are common enough. Such successes are regarded as special cases, dependent on a few talented leaders. The more interesting and formidable challenge is to replicate success for many students in many classrooms across many schools, by improving the performance of many average teachers and administrators. (pp. 342-343)

This book is intended, as we stated in the introduction, to be a resource for administrators, teacher leaders, teachers, and other school personnel who are engaged with the "interesting and formidable challenge" Ferguson described—creating schools filled with classrooms that work well for literally all children. In this chapter, we describe ways in which classroom instruction and classroom climate in equitable and excellent schools differ from the instruction and climate found in schools that are much less successful with diverse students. However, this is not an in-depth chapter on instructional practices, such as cooperative learning groups, differentiated instruction, and so on. Instead, we are trying to raise some possibilities that can assist us in creating equitable and excellent classrooms.

HIGH EXPECTATIONS AND RESPECT

High expectations and *respect* are possibly two of the most overused terms in education today. As was pointed out in the chapter about the importance of beliefs, virtually every school has some form of the mantra-like "all children can learn" in its mission statement. In our work as researchers, we have had the opportunity to visit hundreds of school campuses, and we've never been to one in which the educators did not say they had high expectations for all of their students. Never have we seen a banner on the wall of an entry hall that reads "We Have Low Expectations for Our Students Here!" or a sign in a classroom reading "We Treat Our Students With Disrespect and Disdain Here."

If some sort of truth in advertising law were in effect for public schools, however, many of the schools that we have visited in which large percentages of children failed to achieve high standards would have signs posted saying exactly those things. In contrast, the schools in which all students are experiencing high and equitable success truly have a climate of high expectations and respect for their students that permeates all aspects of school life. This climate of high expectations and respect is translated from the school mission statement into the central focus of each teacher's classroom. Indeed, it is translated into everyone's focus on children, both in the school and in the community.

However, we need to be clear about what this climate of high expectations and respect means in classroom practice. It does not mean patronizing attitudes toward children whose homes may not have high levels of economic resources, and it does not mean lowered academic expectations or avoidance of the content areas in which children may need the most work. It means exactly the opposite. It means teachers seeing children, all children, from an assets-based viewpoint and expecting them to learn challenging academic content. As a veteran teacher said to us in a research interview, "I've come to understand that caring about children means insisting that they learn."

Another important point to emphasize here is that "all means all." In other words, teachers must hold high expectations for and teach every child, not just the best and not just those in the middle. This means that teachers need to be attuned on a daily basis to who is learning what and who is not, and then teachers must find ways to make sure each and every child is learning everything in the curriculum. When a child is not learning everything at the same rate as other children, teachers who are successful with diverse students are persistent and relentless in finding a way for that child to learn. For example, a principal in a highly successful elementary school serving low-income Hispanic children described this as a philosophy of stubborn persistence in finding the right mix for every child (Riester, Pursch, & Skrla, 2002).

However, this stubborn persistence may mean more than what can be done in a single classroom. It may require alternative possibilities, like before or after school tutoring or Saturday academies. It may require structuring the day differently from the traditional model. The point, though, is that there is always a "stubborn persistence" to find an answer that will work so that all kids can learn.

CULTURALLY RESPONSIVE TEACHING

In order to transform into reality the high expectations for academic success that we are advocating—in view of the fact that this is not typically happening at present—most teachers will have to make significant shifts in their viewpoints and will have to learn new pedagogical practices that are better matched to the needs of the children sitting in their classrooms. This means principals and other school leaders have the responsibility for investing in high-quality, sustained professional development to build the capacity of the teachers in their schools to be successful with the students they have.

One area upon which such professional development should rightly focus is on building understanding and expertise in the area of culturally responsive teaching. Ladson-Billings (1994), Delpit (1996), and Gay (2000) are among some of the respected scholars who have articulated frameworks for what culturally responsive teaching is and what it looks like in classroom practice. The basic premise is that teachers should teach using philosophies and methods that respect, value, and use positively the strengths of students' home cultures, contexts, and languages. It is based, as Moll has argued (see Moll, 1992;

see also Gonzalez et al., 1995), on the "funds of knowledge" that all children bring to school with them.

Since the overwhelming majority of the nation's teachers are white females and the nation's students are increasingly students of color, the need for professional development in this area of culturally responsive teaching has never been more acute than it is today. Furthermore, it is important to understand that the large numbers of white female teachers who comprise the majority of our teaching force may not even have neutral perspectives on the dignity, worth, and educability of the children of color and children from low-income homes who inhabit their classrooms. It is an unfortunate fact that many teachers carry (often unconsciously) negative and deficit viewpoints about the children whom they have been charged to educate (see Marx, 2002; McKenzie, 2002).

It is essential that these negative and "subtractive" (see Valenzuela, 1999) views be brought to teachers' awareness and that understanding be built about how to change these views and adopt culturally responsive teaching practices. It may seem as if this point is being overemphasized, but the type of classroom change that has to happen in order for children who have not been well served in the past to have culturally respectful classroom experiences depends for its success on changing teachers' awareness of their own, most often hidden and unexamined, beliefs about the children they teach. The example in Box 4.1, which is based on the real-life experience of one of our principalship students, illustrates the power that such hidden beliefs can have.

Box 4.1

Troy, a middle-aged, white male elementary principal who had just begun work at a new campus, approached his first head principal job with great enthusiasm. The majority of students at his new campus were African

(Continued)

Box 4.1 (Continued)

American and Hispanic and lived in federally subsidized housing complexes in a low-income area of the small city in which the school was located. Troy had spent the three previous school years as assistant principal in a similar elementary school in the same district, a school whose students had made great strides academically during Troy's time there. He knew from this experience that students in his new school could be equally successful, and he knew that changing the belief systems of some of his teachers and developing better relations with parents were two of the keys to starting his school on the path to success.

During a day-long professional development session with his new faculty before the start of the school year, Troy announced that one of his initiatives for the coming school year was to improve the quality and amount of communication and interaction between teachers and parents. To that end, he had set up regularly scheduled evening meetings to be held on site at different housing complexes throughout the school year. These were designed to be informal opportunities for parents and children to interact with teachers and to discuss the children's progress, and meals would be served. Troy informed the staff that all teachers would be required to attend several of these meetings on a rotating basis and that he, along with the assistant principals and counselors, would be in attendance at all of them.

At the end of the day, Troy sat in his office reflecting on the day's events, when Carly, a young white female beginning her first year as a teacher, tapped on his door and asked if he had a minute to talk with her. Troy invited her in and asked what was on her mind. Carly said, "I've come to tell you that I won't be able to attend those meetings at the housing projects."

Troy said, "We have quite a few scheduled on different evenings throughout the year; I'm sure we'll be able to work out a schedule so that you can participate."

Carly replied, "You don't understand." When Troy asked her to elaborate what it was he didn't understand, Carly hesitated a long while and then burst out, "I'm too pretty to go there."

Feeling somewhat stunned by her statement, Troy took several minutes to gather his thoughts and then asked her to explain what she meant by that comment and how she came to think that way. What he learned from the rest of the conversation was that her parents and other members of her family had warned her from childhood that her blond good looks put her in danger of physical attack from men, particularly from African American men, and that she should always be careful never to put herself in a position of vulnerability. So, in this teacher's mind, she could not attend evening meetings at the housing complexes because to do so would put her in danger from the male parents of her students and from other men who might be there.

Because Troy, through his master's studies and through his own lived experiences, had developed some understanding of how deep, often unconscious prejudices against racial groups and socioeconomic classes form and how they drive people's beliefs and behavior, he was able to hear out Carly's explanation without reacting angrily or dismissively. Instead, he let her know straightforwardly that no teachers would be excused from attendance at the evening parent meetings, including her. However, he also let her know that he and the other administrators and her mentor teacher would provide

(Continued)

Box 4.1 (Continued)

---

support and assistance to ensure that her interactions with parents were successful and productive.

By December of that school year, Carly's interactions at the evening meetings with her students' parents, the professional learning opportunities provided by her principal, and dialogues with her mentor teacher had helped Carly come to completely new understandings about her students and their families and had helped her understand her former deficit views of her students and their families for what they were. She eventually became one of the most successful teachers at her campus. Without a principal who was able to understand her fears and who was willing to confront them and to work to change them, however, Carly's first-year teaching experience, and the experiences of the students in her classroom that year, would have been altogether different.

As Troy's story clearly shows, teachers often need to unlearn old beliefs and to learn new, more productive ones in order to successfully teach the children who now sit in their classrooms. Thus, schools must invest in significant, sustained, and integrated professional development efforts centered on culturally responsive teaching to see benefits in not only school and classroom climate but in student achievement as well. The following is an exchange among a group of elementary teachers at a highly successful school (taken from a research interview) that illustrates this point.

[Teacher #1]   For so long it was an idea of "I don't see color, I love everybody" and that's totally not what you're supposed to do. You're supposed to see the diversity, supposed to see the difference—

[Teacher #2]   Appreciate and acknowledge it.

[Teacher #1]   Appreciate it, learn it. There may be some trait of another culture that I'm totally unaware of, but I can see a similar trait in my culture. It's just showing, I think, the kids that we're more alike than we are different, but yet we still celebrate our differences.

[Teacher #3]   Well, I know the children love it [the multicultural curriculum]. [It helps the students] to know that their counterparts may have some different viewpoints than they do. With this diversity [curriculum], we can explain to them that we're all alike, but yet we still have our beliefs and our culture, and they like to see the other cultures. It makes a group here. It's a commitment to the group.

[Teacher #1]   I've just seen students open up more in class. They see that teachers don't expect them all to come in and sit exactly the same way and respond exactly the same way. They feel freer now to be the person that they are and know that they're not going to be punished for it. They may be asked to tone it down a little bit, but they're not going to be scrutinized and expected to all be the same.

These teachers' comments are just one small example of the positive power of culturally responsive teaching. It is truly a way to respect and appreciate our students, and it is assets oriented, rather than deficit oriented.

LOVING AND CARING IN THE CLASSROOM

Nell Noddings (1986, 1992) helped to make caring a respected category in the scholarship on schools. Others have reframed caring and applied this concept to schooling an "unjust world" (Eaker-Rich & Van Galen, 1996; Valenzuela, 1999). However, all along, most teachers have been caring to some students, and some teachers have been caring to all students. Nonetheless, as Ladson-Billings (1994) pointed out so well in *The Dreamkeepers*, teachers who are highly successful with children of color, in our present social and historical context, move up from caring to loving all their children.

Of course, loving anyone is hard work—wonderful, but truly hard, work. Loving our own children, the ones we have raised or are raising, is wonderful, but truly hard work. Thus, for us to suggest that successful teachers of diverse students love all their children is not a light suggestion. It is not even a moderate suggestion. Some children, among any group of children, are not easy to love. Some are going to test every fiber in our bodies and our souls. That's just the way it is.

Nonetheless, loving all the children in our classrooms is just what we are suggesting. It is like a "call" to love, a call to step up to a higher level in what we do. It is a higher calling to love all our children. We know this is not simple or easy, but why set a goal less than this? We are not suggesting that we become white knights to our children or saviors of them. Those are patronizing orientations. We are talking about something else altogether. We are talking about loving them— holding them and ourselves to the highest expectations. Every one of them. No exceptions. No matter how hard it is.

If we do this, we won't ever stop. We won't hold back. We will create the conditions in which every one of our students can learn and succeed. Nothing else will be acceptable to us— because we love them.

DEMOCRATIC, COLLABORATIVE TEACHING ENVIRONMENTS

One of the most common complaints we hear about using standards as tools to improve equity and excellence in schools is the contention that standards inevitably equal standardization of instruction and narrowing of the curriculum. In other words, many educators feel that it is impossible to institute accountability and common standards for learning while preserving classroom environments that value democratic practice and collaborative teaching. In our experience with some of the best schools we've seen, however, this balance between accountability and democratic practice is exactly what they've been able to achieve, and, further, it is one of the things most often cited by the educators at these schools as an example of a practice that supports their high success.

In these schools, the standards for student learning are very clear, and the accountability for achieving results is definitely in place, as an always imperfect but necessary check on learning. The methods by which leaders and teachers go about implementing the standards and achieving the results, though, are based on shared responsibility, democratic decision making, and collaborative planning and instruction. This stands in sharp contrast to more traditional, often ineffective, schools serving diverse children in which teachers go through their days in crushing isolation. Teachers in highly successful schools use the curriculum standards and student work products as foci for ongoing, critically reflective dialogue about their own practice. For example, one teacher at a successful campus described this integration of accountability and teamwork,

> We realize we are here for the students . . . with all the accountability we are responsible, you know, for giving in all realms. We realize that "Hey, I can't do it all by myself" and if I try, I'm going to fall apart so, therefore, here comes vertical teaming, planning, grade level planning, where we say, "Hey, what are you doing that can help me?" and "Let's work together."

Indeed, there is considerable research (see, e.g., Reyes et al., 1999; Senge, 1990; Sergiovanni, 1994) on successful classroom practices that consistently indicates that collaborative practice is an essential part of creating equitable and excellent schooling.

Furthermore, this collaborative model of classroom practice extends beyond planning and dialogue. Leaders and teachers in equitable and excellent schools typically think flexibly and creatively about who teaches what, when, and how. In addition, leaders and teachers in these schools design structures and practices that utilize the expertise of regular teachers, special education teachers, instructional specialists, and teacher teams to make proactive and focused efforts on behalf of kids who have particular instructional needs. Moreover, they do all of this without resorting to labeling and sorting practices so prevalent in traditional models of schooling (see Capper et al., 2000, for an expanded, and excellent, discussion of how this type of flexible practice operates). Furthermore, the focus is not on succeeding on the accountability tests; the goal is student learning, with the test as a necessary but imperfect check on this learning.

CONTINUAL DEVELOPMENT OF CONTENT EXPERTISE

In addition to continually developing good instructional practices, equitable and excellent schools also invest in a continuous program of building teachers' knowledge of the content they are expected to teach. This approach is necessary for two important reasons. First, new teachers most often come from teacher preparation programs with only minimal understanding of their grade level or subject area, especially as these intersect with being successful with children of color and children from low-income families. Certification for these teachers is only a beginning, not an end point. It is thus necessary for schools to recognize that the learning curve for new teachers in their content will be steep. As a result, schools and districts need to build in multiple and ongoing opportunities for professional learning.

Second, curriculum standards and content are ever changing. As states respond to new federal mandates related to standards and assessment, the pace of change will only increase. If teachers are to be well prepared to be successful with all their students in the content for which the students will be held responsible on accountability exams, it is absolutely essential that all teachers, both new and experienced, know the content well themselves.

To be successful, then, each school and district needs to have a plan for constant building of teacher capacity. This applies to all teachers. Typically, we think of improving the capacity of only the weaker teachers. However, to create schools that are successful with diverse students, schools that are constantly improving the achievement of all kids year to year, it is necessary to constantly improve the instructional capacity of all teachers. There is no top end or glass ceiling to quality of teaching, just like there is no top end or glass ceiling for writing or painting; anyone, no matter how good they already are, can always get better.

In addition, in districts that have persistently raised the academic achievement of all children, regardless of students' backgrounds, this professional development is targeted to specific areas of teacher need. We both have spent time observing instructional specialists going out to schools to spend an hour or two helping small groups of teachers learn to become successful in teaching an area of the curriculum that they have been identified as not being successful in. Other districts have assigned curriculum specialists to individual schools, and the responsibility of these specialists is to constantly increase the teaching capacity of everyone in the building by targeting assistance to the particular needs of specific teachers. Whatever approach is used, the point is to target professional development to the specific needs of teachers, given the children in their classrooms. Excellent resource books are available to help leaders design professional development that meets the needs of individual teachers. See, for example, *Designing Professional Development for Teachers of Math and Science* (Loucks-Horsley, Hewson, Love, & Stiles, 1997).

DISCIPLINE PROBLEMS ARE
LARGELY A FUNCTION OF INEQUITY,
A LACK OF CARING, AND WEAK INSTRUCTION

We understand that one of the most common complaints from teachers working in racially and economically diverse schools is the behavior of students. We know that this is one of the most troublesome areas for teachers. We also know that many teachers have not been shown or taught how to create a behaviorally appropriate classroom that serves all students well and that creates the space for good instruction to occur. Rather than blame the students or their parents, as we often do, we need to learn how to create behaviorally appropriate classrooms that serve all students well. There are simply too many teachers who know how to do this, typically some in every school, for the rest of us to continue to not know how to do it.

In our experience, it is a general rule that a classroom or school that is both equitable and excellent does not have many discipline problems. Yes, there are a few individual students with various kinds of serious problems that lead to discipline issues. For example, there may be abuse in the family, just like there is in some middle-class families. As soon as any serious problem is identified, however, a team of teachers, counselors, and administrators who have previously been prepared to assist such students should immediately go into action. They should quickly and caringly investigate the student's problem, work collaboratively with the student's parents or caregivers, develop a range of good solutions, implement the appropriate solution or solutions, monitor the effects, and continue working to provide the best possibilities for the student.

Except for these few students, there should be infrequent discipline problems in schools that serve all children well. In fact, if there are frequent discipline problems in a classroom or school, this should be seen as a problem that the adults have— a system problem, not a student problem. We have visited high schools serving diverse students in which the discipline room is packed, there are five or six professionals dealing with those sent to the discipline room, and these professionals are exhausted and burned out, but the problems don't ever seem to go away. Typically, in these schools, the blame is placed on the students, the parents, or both.

We have also been in schools serving the same type of student population, but where none of the above is occurring. In these latter schools, discipline cases are infrequent and irregular. No professional is burned out with discipline cases, and the students are spending their entire day in classrooms where they can learn. The difference between these two kinds of schools is not in the students or in the capabilities of the professionals. The difference is in the system of the school, the system set up by the leaders in the school and in the assumptions the educators make about themselves and their students.

When we provide caring, respectful, appreciative, high-quality instruction for children, they respond. Thus, discipline problems in general should be seen mainly as evidence that there is something wrong in the way we are operating our classrooms or schools, or in the way we are treating our students. This is even more the case when particular groups of children, like African American boys or Latino boys, are receiving most of the discipline or a disproportionate percentage of the discipline (we will later cover a method you can use to identify and address such problems). When particular groups of students are receiving most of the discipline or a disproportionate percentage of the discipline, this is a telling indication that this is our problem, not the children's. We are doing something very wrong. This, indeed, is inequity at work.

In equitable and excellent schools, two things are true in regard to discipline. The first is that there is almost always an orientation toward classroom behavioral norms that is non-punitive, that establishes appropriate behaviors, and that applies to both students and educators. This last part must be explicit. In other words, not only do these schools establish rules for acceptable student behaviors, disseminate them widely, and deliberately teach them as an integrated part of the curriculum, these schools also establish similar rules for teachers and other educators. The second thing that is true in equitable and excellent schools is that truly engaging all students in learning leads to far fewer problems with discipline. Students know when we truly care about them and are truly committed to their learning. When students know this, they are much less interested in or involved in any disruptive behaviors. In other words, classrooms and schools in which students are really learning simply do not have many discipline problems. This is an intended positive outcome of equitable and excellent classrooms and schools.

CONCLUSION

In this chapter on instruction and classroom climate, we have not tried to provide "how-to's" or, even, discussions of specific kinds of classroom techniques, like collaborative learning or authentic instruction. Instead, we have provided discussions of some areas that we have identified as particularly useful in schools serving children of color and children from low-income families. Even with these, though, we haven't provided in-depth, how-to-do-it advice. What we have provided is some discussion to provoke your thinking about the topics covered and to hopefully spur you on to find out more about them.

We have covered high expectations and respect, along with culturally responsive teaching. We recommended moving from caring for to loving all our students. We discussed democratic, collaborative teaching environments. We talked about continuous professional development of content expertise and the systematic targeting of that development to specific teachers serving specific students. Finally, we addressed discipline issues, both the way they are typically addressed and the different way they are addressed in successful schools serving diverse children. As in the rest of this book, our purpose is not to give you a detailed plan but to facilitate and provoke your thinking about how to create equitable and excellent classrooms, schools, and districts that truly serve all children well.

In the next chapter, we address accountability and data usage. We realize that especially the first of these, accountability, is controversial with many educators, education scholars, parents, and policymakers. Indeed, we know many are completely against accountability as presently construed. However, our frame will be that we can and need to positively use accountability to serve the creation of equitable and excellent schools.

CHAPTER FIVE

Accountability and Appropriate Data Usage

> *Never in the history of human civilization has a society attempted to educate* all *of its children [emphasis added]. Under this new law, we will strive to provide every boy and girl in America with a high-quality education—regardless of his or her income, ability, or background.*
>
> —Rod Paige (2002),
> U.S. Secretary of Education

W hether Secretary Paige in his statement above was serious or not, whether his statement was meant as rhetoric or reality, and whether his historical assessment was hyperbole or fact, the two of us strongly believe that in this country we need to provide every boy and girl with "a high quality education—regardless of his or her income, ability, or background." Indeed, this is the focus of this entire book. However, what Paige and the Bush administration typically symbolize, even though it did not start with them, even in Texas, is accountability.

Here, then, is what we believe to be the truth about state accountability systems and the tests on which they are based. All accountability tests are samples of a domain of subject knowledge, like math or biology. Also, all tests are based on some kind of theory about knowing and learning, such as, for example, behaviorism, constructivism, or some mixture of theories. However, there is no agreement or consensus among scholars and experts as to which theory is the correct one, and there may never be. Moreover, even if we all agreed on what the correct theory is, this would likely not mean that we would necessarily agree on how to correctly sample a particular knowledge domain or on what the correct way to test knowledge of that domain is.

Furthermore, all tests have culture and history (i.e., biases) built into them. There is no such thing as a culture-free, history-free, bias-free test. All tests are embedded in the viewpoints or perspectives (all of which can be called *biases*) of the societies, the cultures, and the histories from which the tests emerge. Indeed, the very idea of using tests to check knowledge and skills is itself a cultural bias, that is, some cultures would never use a "test" to check knowledge and skills. Thus, from the beginning, it is important to recognize that there are no absolutely appropriate, unbiased, perfect accountability tests. They are all conditional; they are all just attempts; they are all biased; they are all imperfect. Nonetheless, this does not mean that we cannot constantly improve these tests in various ways. We always can and we always should. In fact, some scholars, such as Carl Glickman (2001), argue that this constant struggle to test and improve our educational methods, including the tests themselves, is, and should be, a foundational principle of American education.

Thus, even the fact that we know accountability tests are not perfect and may have many problems does not mean that accountability tests are not useful. In fact, our view is that they are highly useful for developing equitable and excellent schools. When we are trying to educate millions of students, we need a way to mark the student learning that we either are or are not accomplishing. In addition, when we have the kind of inequities by specific student groups, like racial groups, that we currently have, we need a way to mark those differences and to mark the erasure of those differences—when we attain equity.

In fact, in working with people, especially with their minds and their emotions, we never have markers that are perfect. We almost always must work with imperfect markers, like our accountability tests. That is acceptable for now. When we get to a level in our educational system at which accountability tests are no longer meaningful or appropriate, if we ever do, we will move on to something else. Right now, though, we strongly believe, and our research and that of many others shows, that these accountability markers are necessary to creating equitable and excellent schools (see, e.g., a dialogue we have had with others on these issues in the following three articles in the order that they appeared in *Phi Delta Kappan:* Scheurich et al., 2000; Valencia, Valenzuela, Sloan, & Foley, 2001; Scheurich & Skrla, 2001).

However, in this book, we are *not* going to provide an extended argument for why accountability measures are important. If you do want to read our arguments in this regard, and responses from some of our critics, our work and that of our critics is listed in the reference list at the end of this book (specifically, see the citations in the preceding paragraph plus Haney, 2001; Klein, 2001; Skrla, Scheurich, Johnson, & Koschoreck, 2001a, 2001b; and the entire issue of the journal *Education and Urban Society*, Vol. 33, No. 3, edited by Skrla, Scheurich, & Johnson, 2001). However, no matter whether your perspective totally differs from ours, has some agreement with ours, or is in total agreement with ours, we strongly believe that on this large, controversial, and conflicted issue, everyone ought to be willing to engage with an open mind the whole range of arguments and research. Accountability is a highly complex topic, and there is good research on its effects that people on all sides of the issue can point to for support. Thus, simply saying you are for or against accountability is probably not a useful or informed position to take.

Another important issue in this area is that all state accountability systems are not created equal (see, e.g., Linn et al., 2002). Indeed, there is a huge amount of variation among such systems, although the very recent passage of the federal *No Child Left Behind Act*—which requires annual accountability testing—will definitely force more standardization across states. A further issue is that the quality of these systems varies tremendously. Moreover, these accountability systems usually change annually, from a little to a lot depending on the decisions of state legislatures and state education agencies. Despite this variability among states, despite the fact that some state systems have a lower quality, and despite the annual changes, we recommend, as we did with standards, that you work out how to use the accountability systems positively—which is what we will discuss below.

Avoiding the Test Factory Response to Accountability

What we emphatically do not recommend is what has been called turning your school into a "test factory" (see Ashby, 2000). Unfortunately, this is how some districts, schools, principals, and teachers adapt to accountability tests. They turn classroom instruction into almost year-round test prep. Curriculum and instruction in these schools narrows to the point that only what is measured by the test is taught. We consider this not only to be unprofessional, but, even more important, to be an ethical and moral violation. Let's make it more dramatic: *To turn your district, school, or classroom into a test factory is unquestionably wrong, unethical, unprofessional, and immoral.* It is a violation at the deepest level of the very idea of public education in a democracy and the very idea of teaching as a profession. Even more important, though, it sells children short; it betrays them to the needs of adults who are seeking to merely appear that they are succeeding.

Some will argue that accountability systems literally force schools to become test factories and that a test factory school is the only way to be successful within some state accountability systems. We strongly disagree with this. We have studied too many successful classrooms and schools serving diverse students that do *not* do this in a state well known for its tough, high-stakes accountability system to believe that test prep is the only way to succeed. Thus, we know it is possible to use accountability systems positively. We also know that it is possible to create equitable and excellent schools in which real student learning is occurring within tough, high-stakes accountability systems.

This does not mean that there aren't classrooms, schools, and districts in which educators believe that becoming a test factory is the best way, the only way, or the fastest way to succeed in a high-stakes accountability system. There are many of these. There are also many classrooms, schools, and districts in which there is success at a high level with any student population you can name—inner city, poverty dominated, rural, multiracial, and so on—but they have not become test factories.

Again, we want to strongly emphasize that becoming a test factory, turning a major portion of the school year over to preparation for a specific test, is wrong, wrong, wrong—ethically, professionally, morally. It is a flat-out, total betrayal of our children.

Using Accountability Positively for Equitable and Excellent Schooling

The appropriate goal of accountability is to ensure that students are learning your standards and your curriculum, as we discussed in the last chapter. The appropriate goal is for real student learning to be occurring—learning in the knowledge and skills areas designated by your standards.

Nonetheless, it is also important to understand that you can have a specified curriculum (and good standards), that you can have all teachers focused on their part in this curriculum, and that you can have all teachers for a particular grade and subject operating on the same time frame. This, however, does not mean that you will necessarily be on the road to creating an equitable and excellent school.

Why? Here is one of the really key differences between equitable and excellent schools and most other schools, even the ones that are considered "good" or "excellent" schools. In most schools—using what we might call the old model or old paradigm—a teacher would teach a subject and expect that a few students would do really well, most would do acceptably well, and some would do poorly. In this "old paradigm," teachers thought that how well their students learned was largely due to the students themselves. If the students had the right preparation at home, had the right attitude (learned at home), good work habits (learned at home), and a decent intelligence (in the genes), those students would do reasonably well.

Again, we want to say that this is a really key point. In equitable and excellent schools, this is *not* how it works. There is what we might call a new model or new paradigm. In equitable and excellent schools, the goal of the whole school is to get *each and every* child, no matter what his or her differences are and no matter what he or she has learned or not learned at home, to learn the designated curriculum material at the highest level. This obviously is a very different perspective for educators to have. This obviously requires that teachers learn how to work in a very different way than they did under the old paradigm.

Think of a specific classroom filled with a typical group of children—girls and boys, children from different races and cultures, children from homes with different incomes, and children with different kinds of abilities. Under this new approach, the job of the whole school is to help every one of the children reach a high level of learning. We are not, please note, saying the approach is to help all children "reach their highest potential," as many commonly say. We are, instead, saying that each child will learn whatever is in the curriculum at the highest level. As we said, this *is* a different paradigm.

Some people call these kinds of schools high performance schools. The label "high performance" comes from the scholarly area called organizational studies. There exist, then, what are called high performance organizations (for more on these, see, e.g., Lawler, Mohrman, & Benson, 2001, among many others). In these organizations, people are not thought of as lined up along a bell curve, with a few being low performing, many in the middle, and a few being at the highest performance levels. Instead, in these high performance organizations, it is assumed that the leadership will create the kind of organization climate, culture, employee assistance and support, training, and whatever else necessary so that *all* personnel will perform at the highest level.

In these organizations, there is no assumption that a person will not perform at the highest levels because the individual is a person of color, a female, a person with a disability, or a person from a lower income family, from an immigrant family, or from a home in which the home language is not English. The expectation is simply to create an organization that supports everyone becoming a high performer.

This is what we are talking about with equitable and excellent schools—every student performs at the highest levels. Our job, then, as educators is to create the educational conditions for this to happen. If, for example, the curriculum requires that students learn two-digit multiplication, we are saying our job as a school is to figure out a way to teach this material so that all children, no matter their differences, no matter what their home life is like, will learn how to perform this skill at the highest level. In this new paradigm, what it means to be an educator is that you know how to work collaboratively with other educators, parents, and community members to create a classroom or school in which each and every child learns at the highest level each of the areas of knowledge and each skill that is in your curriculum.

Please think about this for a moment because this is really critical. The whole idea of equitable and excellent schools rests on this. The old paradigm of the bell curve in which only a few do well, most do OK, and some fail needs to be gotten rid of. It is not a truth; it is nothing but a socially created and maintained concept. Instead, we all need to learn how to work collaboratively with other educators, parents, and community members to be successful with each and every child in each and every subject and grade. This is not going to happen in one step or one year, but a clear pattern of progress in this direction can be established in two to three years. If this is what we need to do, then, of course, each teacher must understand that she or he cannot accomplish this all by herself or himself. This is going to require a team effort—deep collaboration among students, teachers, administrators, other experts, student families, and the whole community.

At the beginning of a change effort, with most teachers in most classrooms, the teacher will easily be highly successful with some students—let's say 33%. With another 33%, let's say, a teacher, learning from other teachers and experts in his or her school, can learn how to be highly successful. To achieve success with the final 33% is going to take some deeper effort, some more substantive learning, some willingness to really change how we see teaching and learning, some creativity that perhaps exceeds the normal classroom arrangement of one teacher with one set of students, some real ongoing work with others. It may even require after-school or Saturday work, or it may require changing the structure of the day to serve this final 33% of students. However, this can be done. Educators are smart, imaginative people. If we are committed to figuring out how to be successful with every child, we can be successful with every child, and this is one place that accountability is important.

Even though accountability tests are limited, as we noted at the beginning of this chapter, we believe we need them for this effort to be highly successful with all students. We need to have some reasonable, workable ways to determine by teacher, by school, by district, and by state which of our students are successfully learning our curriculum and which of them are not—particularly, which *groups* of students are not. We also need some standardization of the means of determining learning success across classrooms, schools, districts, and states. This is very important in creating equitable and excellent schools because typically there are some groups of children, such as children of color, children from low-income families, children from cultures other than the white middle-class culture, children in which the home or first language is not English, and so on, with whom we have persistently not been as successful. Accountability gives us a useful check on this. This, in fact, is one of the areas that accountability has been most useful to schools and districts that have responded to the challenges of equity and excellence. That is, accountability has revealed the inequities produced by traditional methods of schooling, and it has pushed some districts to really take on the challenge of facilitating the learning of all children.

State accountability tests are usually given once a year, and this check on our success is important, even with all of the limitations of these tests. However, our research (see, e.g., Skrla et al., 2000) has clearly shown that equitable and excellent schools go much further than this. Remember that these successful schools have a timed schedule for their curriculum. They have all teachers teaching a particular subject in a particular grade at close to the same time. They have these teachers in collaboration with each other, working together to make the whole team, every teacher, successful.

In these schools, then, at certain intervals—it may be every two weeks, it may be every month, but it is never longer than every six weeks—there is an accountability check done on student learning. These checks are usually teacher-designed tests or tasks that all of the students in a particular subject, grade, or both, are given at about the same time, if not the same day. The tests or tasks assess student command of the specific curriculum material (or curriculum standards) that the teachers were covering during the time period in question. If done every two weeks, the checks (multiple choice, authentic, performance—whatever is appropriate) are usually very short, maybe less than ten questions or a few performance tasks. If done every six weeks, the checks are usually longer. In every case, however, the checks cover the specific knowledge and skills domain that is being taught by all the teachers during the particular time period in question. Sometimes these tests or tasks mimic the state's accountability tests in their type of questions and format; sometimes they do not; and sometimes they are a mix. However, each teacher does not make up her or his own test; typically all the teachers teaching the same thing at about the same time use the same test or tasks.

Each teacher carefully examines the results for each child, with the goal of understanding what story the tests tell about how well each child learned what was taught. Typical questions that guide this type of analysis of test score data include the following:

Which children did well on very few test questions or tasks?

What was the problem in each case?

Which children got about half right?

What was the problem in each case?

Which questions were missed by the children who got most of the questions right?

Why did this happen?

What are the patterns of right and wrong answers by individual and group?

What needs to be done for each child and for each student group to bring them all to high levels of success?

How does the classroom environment need to be changed?

How do student interactions need to be changed?

How do student-teacher interactions need to be changed?

What does a specific teacher need to learn to do differently?

These are examples of the kinds of questions that each teacher needs to ask in examining the test results. The point with all of these questions is that the teacher-designed tests or performance tasks data become an ongoing basis for checking student learning and for figuring out how to improve instruction so that every child is learning the material to the highest level. In the old paradigm, the teacher simply assumed the reason some students learned and some did not was a function of the students themselves. In this new approach, every teacher assumes that the reason some students do not learn is a function of teaching technique, classroom climate, materials, or some other definable, correctable variable. In the new paradigm, the focus has shifted to how to provide the educational conditions for each and every child to learn at the highest level.

It does not stop here, however. The teachers teaching the same subject and grade need to focus team time on their results. The type of questions that would be useful in guiding this collaborative analysis include the following:

What insights can the group share?

What possible solutions can individuals offer to each other?

What outside help is needed?

Does the entire group, some of the group, or just one member of the group need some specific professional development?

Are there patterns of lack of learning or of success across all members of the team?

Are some students, such as middle-class white students, learning well, while other students, such as Latino students, are not?

Are boys learning better than girls or vice versa? What do the patterns mean?

In all cases, all of the team needs to take responsibility not just for his or her students, but also for all students served by the team. All of the team needs to work very hard to help all of the team be successful with all of the students.

The following exchange between an elementary teacher and a research interviewer illustrates the importance of this collaborative approach to addressing the needs revealed by test data:

[Researcher]   What do you all do if you feel like you're having problems teaching a certain kind of skill, that it's a problem *you're* having rather than a specific child's problem?

[Teacher]   Go to my fellow teachers and ask what they're doing. Like spelling. The other teacher, her kids were making good grades and mine weren't, so I just went to her and said, "What are you doing? I need help." We just work together, get other ideas.

[Researcher]   In this specific case, what did you learn that the other teacher was doing differently than you were?

[Teacher]   Making it more exciting, spelling. I think spelling [is] very exciting to me, but there are ways to make it more exciting to the kids, I guess, and just give them more experiences with the words. They made big improvements.

Collaborative data analysis and instructional planning based on it does not stop at the teacher level either. The data on these tests need to go to the school administrators. They need to know what level of learning is going on in each teacher's class. They need to be paying close attention to the success or lack of success of individual teachers, to the success or lack of success of each team, and to the success or lack of success of the whole school. The job of administrators is to ensure that all of the students in their schools learn the entire curriculum at the highest level.

Consequently, administrators need to be asking similar questions. The following are some sample questions to guide administrator analysis of test data:

Which individual teachers are evidencing low levels of success?

With which kids?

Why?

What do the teachers need to get better?

Do they need a mentor?

Are they having trouble with particular student groups or particular areas of the curriculum?

What can be provided to help them improve?

Which teams of teachers are working, helping each other get better?

Why?

Which are not?

Why?

What needs to be done to help the teams improve as teams?

What has been described here, of course, is what some have called a "learning community" (see, among many others writing about this, Reyes et al., 1999; Senge, 1990; Sergiovanni, 1994). It is a group of educators, preferably a whole school, dedicated to learning as a group how to get better, how to be successful with all children at the highest levels. It is a relentless, collaborative effort of the whole school to be successful with each and every student. It is not, though, a one-step process. It is an ongoing, continuous effort to help everyone, from the best to the weakest teachers, to get better and better with each and every child.

In the very best districts, those where the whole district is on the path to creating equitable and excellent schools, this ongoing data collection moves from the teacher to the team to the school administrator to the district administration so that the district leadership can attend both to school and district patterns and determine ways to support individual teachers, groups of teachers, whole schools, or groups of schools. In the best of districts, then, this enterprise of being successful with each and every child in the district is the work and commitment of every educator in the district.

If, then, we are truly doing these kinds of things, what kind of evidence should we expect to see in our accountability data? Some scholars have talked about the volatility of year-to-year data in individual schools (e.g., Linn & Haug, 2002), but we have found in our studies that those schools and districts that are progressing toward becoming equitable and excellent exhibit a clear year-to-year pattern of improvement. The way this pattern looks is that across a large range of measures, such as test scores in different subjects and grades, student retention rates, student attendance rates, and so on, there is a clear indication of year-to-year improvement. This does not mean that every piece of data every year fits the pattern of general improvement, but it does mean that across a whole set of data the pattern of improvement is unquestionable. In addition, our research shows that a general pattern of improvement is usually fairly clear by the second or third year.

We want to be very clear, then, about what we mean on this last point. We do not mean that you pick out some data that shows improvement, emphasize that, and de-emphasize the rest. You need to be rigorously honest about the whole range of data. If you are constantly getting a mixed pattern, then that is *not* a general pattern of improvement. If a significant number of your indicators are staying the same or going down, or going up one year and then down the next, this is not a general pattern of improvement. Again, our research has shown that fairly quickly, in just two or three years, the schools that succeed evidence a general, easily identifiable pattern of improvement across a broad range of data.

If you are not getting a general, ongoing pattern of improvement, you need to ask some hard questions about your process for improvement, really push yourself, and not accept rationalizations. It is highly likely that something is missing, that you are fooling yourself about what you think you are doing, that you are focusing on the wrong things, and so on. It is like being a coach in a sport: If you are not winning, you badly need to rethink your strategies and tactics. Or, if you are a manager of a business that is not being successful, you badly need to rethink your strategies and tactics. In fact, you need to be ruthless with your dedication to success and thus be strongly unwilling to fool yourself or rationalize that you are succeeding when you are not. You must be strongly committed to accepting only one result: a school or a classroom that is on a continuously improving pattern of equitable and excellent academic results.

This focus on accountability needs to pervade the entire system. At all levels, from the individual teacher, teams of teachers, the school leadership, and district leadership to the superintendent, the school board, parents, and the community at large—all must be concerned about and focused on improving student learning for all students, with accountability being but the imperfect measure of this. In the best districts, all levels are using this data to attend to equity and excellence in an ongoing way, not to judge people, but to see where the problems are and then to figure out solutions. Most educators, administrators, or teachers, if given strong support and the assistance they need, are able to become much, much better at their work. Yes, a few may need to decide that education is not their calling. Yes, a few may be unwilling to give up negative stereotypes about some children, but these are only a very few. Virtually all people, if provided with the right circumstances, the right support and professional development, are willing to change and to improve their ability to be successful at their work.

CONCLUSION

Of course, all districts will not be like this. It may be that an individual school will need to undertake this focus on accountability on its own, and many have successfully done so. Our point is that it is necessary to regularly collect data on learning every few weeks, to analyze the meaning of that data, to use the data to target areas that need improvement, and then to carry through on getting the support or training or whatever it is that teachers need in order to be successful with all of the children in their classrooms. Actually, you can even do this as a single teacher, and we have seen this done. However, when people start noticing your success, they will probably come around wanting to know what you are doing.

Of course, people will come to see your success whether you are a successful teacher, school, or district. As our research was ongoing in one district and as we saw that this was a district on the move toward equity and excellence districtwide, we told the district leadership that once our report was published and publicized, they would become famous. They didn't believe us at the time, but later they told us we were right. They are now getting visitors from all over the country. If you are successful, this will likely happen to you until being equitable and excellent is the national norm. That is our goal. We hope by this time that it is your goal too.

In the next chapter we will discuss using accountability data and other data we already routinely collect to root out systemic patterns of inequity that are barriers to creating equitable and excellent schools. These are barriers to equitable and excellent schools that are internal to the school, part of the school's own system. Using a label others originated, we refer to the efforts to identify and address these patterns of inequity as *equity audits*.

CHAPTER SIX

Using Data to Uncover and Erase Systemic Inequities

As an administrator, I set out on my own quest to gather more data and research to show that Black kids and poor kids were just as capable as middle-income White kids. Working along with other administrators who were willing to take risks, we examined patterns of tracking and opportunities to take mathematics and advanced placement courses. We used the power of data to uncover practices that disenfranchise children and to confront people with the harm they were doing. And we found that we could change people's attitudes and practices.

—Ruth Johnson (1996, p. 274), *Setting Our Sights: Measuring Equity in School Change*

Remember in an earlier chapter where we were discussing causes for the achievement gap between white middle-class children and children of color or children from low-income families? We talked about the various external causes of this gap that educators usually give as explanations for it. Well, here we are going to talk about some internal causes. By internal, we mean causes for the achievement gap that come from inside schools rather than outside or external to them. Unfortunately, educators have not typically talked about these, but if we are going to create equitable and excellent schools, we have to do so.

We call these internal causes of inequity *systemic inequities* because they are built systematically into the processes and procedures of the system that is the school (Scott, 2001). That is, they have become part of the way we typically do schooling, part of our norms. We call the processes that we recommend for addressing these systemic inequities *equity audits*. By equity audits, we mean using district, school, and classroom data to identify, address, and remove systemic patterns of inequity that come from inside the school. Thus, we are talking about auditing data on your classroom, school, or district to identify patterns of inequity for the purpose of addressing those patterns and creating new patterns of equity.

Research we have done (see Skrla, Garcia, Scheurich, & Nolly, 2002) indicates that the idea of equity audits for schools and school districts has a history based in three different arenas. One of these sources is the U.S. civil rights movement. Some in the civil rights movement have devised in-depth, detailed examinations of all the equities and inequities in a district, from the racial makeup of the teachers and the school board to the race of students who dominate high track and low track classes.

These are very thorough examinations that can be highly useful if there is the will to address the issues raised. These types of audits are conducted by private consultants and are similar to reviews done by the U.S. Department of Education Office for Civil Rights when there are suspected civil rights violations in schools and districts. The audits often occur as a result of conflict around racial issues in communities, but then the will to follow through and address the issues raised often disappears as time passes. This is very unfortunate because the audits are often very insightful and very thorough analyses of the equities and inequities in a district. The main problem we have with these equity audits in our work is that they usually produce so many areas of inequity so quickly that it makes it difficult to move from each area of data on inequities to equity solutions. That is, the thorough level of detail often overwhelms any possibility of devising and implementing pragmatic steps for addressing the inequities in a district or school. Therefore, later in the chapter, we make recommendations for more focused and more manageable ways for school leaders to conduct equity audits of their own schools.

A second source of equity audits comes out of the work of curriculum audits. Curriculum audits have been useful tools in school reform for the last two decades. The concepts and methodology for these have been described and operationalized by Fenwick English, William Poston, Betty Steffy, and Jacqueline Mitchell, among others. Curriculum audits usually have to do with making sure that there is a logical, specified curriculum and that this curriculum is aligned grade to grade and subject level to subject level. We discussed some of this and its importance in a prior chapter. Some of those doing this work also devised what they labeled as *equity audits* (see Mitchell & Poston, 1992). In these, they looked at inequities in terms of the curriculum. However, as far as we can determine, while there may be some individuals still doing this kind of work, discussions of it in the research literature virtually disappeared in the early 1990s.

A third stream of thought about equity auditing has appeared more recently in some state departments of education as part of the standards-based reform movement of the last decade. At least two states, Washington and Kentucky, have developed state instruments to assist districts and schools with equity auditing (see www.kde.state.ky.us/ohre/equity/instrument/inst01.asp for Kentucky's Equity Analysis and Data Gathering Instrument). In other states, such as Iowa, the state education department conducts its own equity audits of districts within the state.

Consequently, given the diverse history of the term *equity audit*, we cannot claim that we originated it, but we do use it somewhat differently than others have. First, schools and districts, as a function of accountability measures and other state and federal requirements, now collect a tremendous, and growing, amount of data. Second, fairly recently, much of this data has become publicly available on Web sites and can be downloaded for further analyses by anyone. Third, while there have long been discussions of educational inequity, especially by scholars of color, equity and the achievement gap have really come to the foreground as a major issue in public discussions of education only in the last decade. What we are recommending, then, is to use the data that schools and districts already collect to identify systemic patterns of inequity internal to the school, patterns that prevent, or form barriers to, our being equally successful with all student groups.

APPLYING EQUITY AUDITS TO GIFTED AND TALENTED PROGRAM DATA

Let's start by remembering that our goal is equitable and excellent schools. We want all children to be learning at the highest level; we want high performance for all. Now, let's take one area of schooling, gifted and talented (GT) classes or AP classes—all of those classes that serve the highest achieving students. Disaggregate your GT or AP classes by race and income of the children's families. We are sure you already know or will immediately see the nature of the results of this disaggregation. These advanced classes are overwhelmingly filled with white middle-class students, unless you have none of these students in your school. Even if you only have children of color in your school, typically your GT or AP classes, if you have any of these advanced courses at all, are predominantly populated with children of color from the middle class. Your school may be an exception, but what we have just described as typical is the norm nationwide (Ford & Harmon, 2001).

We will use some specific data to illustrate this point. The data in Figure 6.1 are taken from an urban district we are familiar with.

Figure 6.1   Example District Family Income Inequity in GT

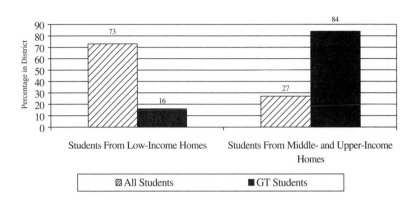

The district has about 50,000 students, with 4,650 in GT courses districtwide, or 9.3% of their student population. Seventy-three percent of the student population, or 36,500 students, come from low-income families. However, there are only 734 students from these low-income families in GT courses in this district. This means that 73% of the districts' students (36,500 students, those from low-income families) supplies only 15.8% of the GT students. As a result, students from low-income families are considerably underrepresented in GT classes.

There is, then, a pattern of inequity that exists inside this district. However, some might respond that this pattern just reflects the skills and knowledge of the kids, so this pattern does have an external cause. Remember, though, that we are talking about creating equitable and excellent schools and districts. We are talking about a new paradigm in which all children and all groups of children by race and income perform equally well. One thing, then, that having an equitable school or district has to mean is that all student groups are equally represented in GT classes, otherwise one cannot claim that all groups are succeeding at high levels. Indeed, how can we have *no* achievement gap among different races and income groups without having proportionate representation in GT classes and all groups succeeding equally in these classes? That is, one thing that eliminating the achievement gap means is that all gifted and talented classes, all honors classes, all AP classes, schoolwide and districtwide, must evidence equal proportions of students by race and family income. In the example we are highlighting here, then, for this district to be equitable, somewhere near 73% of the students in GT classes would be from low-income families, and about 73% of the students succeeding in these GT classes would be from these same families.

Think about who is in your GT classes. To truly have equitable and excellent schools and districts means that all student groups, whether they are students of color, students from low-income families, students from homes where English is not the first language, and so forth, are proportionately represented in GT classes according to their proportions in your school. For example, if 25% of your students are from homes in which English is not the first language, 25% of your GT students should be from this group, and 25% of the students who succeed in GT classes should be from this same group. This is what we mean by proportionate representation. Whatever proportion these different groups comprise in your student population, they should have the same proportion in GT classes if what you are trying to create is an equitable and excellent school or district.

Let's look at a racial disaggregation of who is in the GT classes in the district example we used above (see Figure 6.2). For the district's 50,000 students, 44.8% are Latino, 16.5% are African American, 35.9% are white, and 2.8% are a variety of other racial groups. As we mentioned before, 9.3% of the 50,000 students in the district are in GT classes. However, only 5.8% of the Latino students are in GT; 2.0% of the African American students are in GT; and 15.9% of the white students are in GT.

To have an equitable and excellent district, the district would need to set a target percentage for GT. Let's say the

Figure 6.2   Example District Racial Inequity in GT

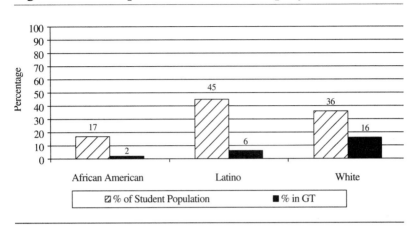

district sets a target of 10% of all students should be in GT. This means that 10% of the Latino students, 10% of the African American students, and 10% of the white students should be in GT. In contrast, in the present situation, both Latino and African American students are significantly underrepresented in GT classes in this district, whereas white students are significantly overrepresented.

Let's look at students in this same example district whose home or first language is not English. Within the overall student population, 15.8% of the students in the district are designated LEP (Limited English Proficient), but only 1.7% of the district's LEP students are in GT. This means that LEP students are also substantially underrepresented. Instead of 1.7% of the GT students being LEP students, 15.8% of the GT students should be LEP students.

Again, some may say that schools themselves can do nothing about which students are in GT, thus leaving the cause for this inequity outside of, or external to, schools. To begin to understand, though, how it is that who gets into GT is under the control or influence of educators within the school, think about your GT entrance criteria, which schools and districts usually establish; think about in which grades students start getting shunted toward GT; think about which parents know to, and know how to, intercede to get their children into GT; and think about how many places there are along a student's path to GT at which unconscious prejudices can enter into the process. For instance, on this last point, it is useful to ask whether your GT criteria are culturally biased so that they favor the culture of some groups of students over the cultures of other groups of students. One example of this is that some cultures devalue individual competition. (For those who say that students need to learn individual competition because that is the way this society works, school is really the main place where this is true, because today the business world tends to require group work over individual work.)

Actually, we have studied schools and districts that have decided to address this problem internally. They have, first, studied those "think abouts" we just mentioned above. They have often found that their GT criteria prevented many talented kids from getting in. They have often found that kids get selected for the GT track early on, frequently in elementary school, and they often found that their old GT criteria unintentionally favored some student groups over other student groups. Therefore, any attempts to address the inequities that influence which students get into GT and which students succeed in GT have to focus on that beginning point in the selection process. Also, these schools and districts have found that middle-class parents often are more aggressively interceding on their children's behalf to get them into GT and that low-income parents and parents of color do not know that this kind of intercession is typical or needed.

In their efforts to achieve equity in GT, the school or district has become more aggressive at contacting parents of color and low-income parents and more aggressive at seeing that their children get into GT. Finally, schools and districts trying to address this issue have found that there are many, many points in the process at which teachers' and administrators' own subjective biases can unwittingly enter in, resulting in some kids not being supported for GT. Most important, though, these schools and districts have found that GT inequities can be successfully addressed internally and that, step by step, schools and districts can make significant strides in making GT equitable—without sacrificing excellence. Later in this chapter, we will go over a general process you can use to find solutions to internal inequities uncovered by an equity audit.

USING EQUITY AUDITS ON SPECIAL EDUCATION DATA

Let's look at another possible area for equity auditing. Let's look at special education assignment. First, for this area you need to know that national experts say that about 10% to 12% of your student population probably requires special education designations. Anything above this indicates overassignment, meaning that some of those assigned to special education don't belong there or that we are using special education assignments to solve other problems (Artiles, 1998). Anything below 10% to 12% indicates underassignment, meaning some students who need special education services are not getting them. (We realize that those who are more familiar with this area will know that to thoroughly address the special education issue, it is necessary to look at every specific special education designation, such as LD [learning disabled] or ED [emotionally disabled]. Nonetheless, to illustrate applying equity audits to special education, we are going to look at the special education data on a general basis.)

Let's disaggregate the data from the example district we are using (see Figure 6.3). Remember that we have a 50,000-student urban district in which 73.0% of the students, or 36,500, come from low-income families. In addition, 44.8% are Latino, 16.5% are African American, 35.9% are white, and 2.8% are from a variety of other racial groups. Within the district, 12.3% of the students are in special education. At first glance, this looks pretty good, as this percentage falls within the range suggested by national experts. However, disaggregating this

Figure 6.3   Percentage of Students in Example District Served in Special Education

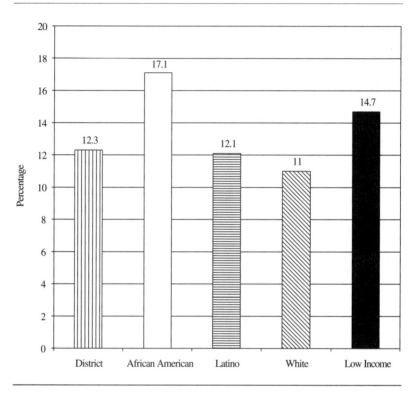

district's data shows that there are again significant patterns of inequity. Among white students, 11.0% are in special education, which is in the proper range. Among Latino students, 12.1% are in special education, also in the correct range. However, 17.1% of the African American students and 14.7% of the students from low-income families are in special education. These latter two figures indicate that there are some inequities in this district. Both of these figures indicate overassignment to special education, meaning there are African American children and children from low-income families who are being assigned to special education but do not belong there. This means that the district is using special education, in the case of the overassignments, for something it was not designed for. In our view, it is unethical and unprofessional to assign children to special education services for reasons different from those that the services were designed for.

Although this is not true of our example district, in some schools and districts, when the data are disaggregated by student group, it will be found that there is underassignment for some groups. ESL students, in particular, are often underassigned to special education services, often because of staff's unfamiliarity with the student's language or a lack of appropriate tools in the student's language. Thus, our deficiencies or deficits, not theirs, often mean that these students are not getting the services they need. Whatever the group, though, underassignment means that there are students in the group who need special education services but are not getting them. This is just as important an inequity pattern as is overassignment.

USING EQUITY AUDITS ON DISCIPLINE

A third area for equity auditing is discipline. The research has repeatedly shown that certain students, particularly African American boys and Latino boys, are receiving a highly disproportionate share of discipline assignments, especially of the most severe discipline designations (see, e.g., "Bridge the Gap," 1997; Pappas & Lucero, 1995-1996; Townsend, 2000). This can readily be seen by looking at some actual data in Figure 6.4. This discipline data is from an urban high school in a district that claims to be strongly committed to equity. The data cover all discipline referrals of any formal kind.

This school is about 10% African American, 50% Latino, and 40% white. However, African American students are receiving 22.3% of the total discipline referrals, over twice their percentage in the general student population of this school. Latinos get 48.6% of the discipline referrals, which is very close to proportionate. Whites get 30.5%, also disproportionate. The data indicate that there are some serious equity problems in this high school.

Figure 6.4   Example High School Racial Inequity in Discipline

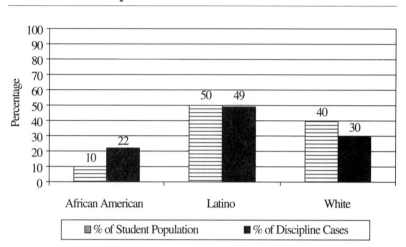

We know many will look at these figures and say that this is just the way things are in an urban high school, that African American and Latino boys do commit higher percentages of disciplinary infractions. By saying this, though, we are implying that the problem is external to education and that we adults who run the educational system have no control over this. However, this is just like GT. We can see this as an internal problem that we can solve. Just like with our discussion of GT above, a clear, thoughtful, objective investigation of how the disproportionate application of discipline to African American and Latino boys occurs will identify areas in which we can institute changes that will increase equity in this area of schooling.

Perhaps a comparison will help. In one high school serving a significant percentage of students of color that one of us studied, the discipline room was large and full of students every day. Five staff members worked all day on discipline cases, and each one had so many students to work with daily that the staff was nearing burnout. In a different but very similar high school serving similar students in a similar urban context, no single staff member focused on discipline all day, and discipline cases were infrequent. The difference was not the students; both schools had largely similar student bodies coming from largely similar contexts. The difference was decisions the staff had made about how the school worked, what the climate was, what the rules and procedures were, and so forth. The fact is that many schools serving any kind or group of students have figured out how to create a school in which discipline is a small issue, not a large one. This difference is in the hands of the adults, not the students.

If we have a school with high numbers of discipline cases, especially if there are disproportionalities, we really need to think about whether there are patterns in the school that may reveal some underlying problems—that is, teacher and administrator attitudes and biases, failures to positively understand African American or Latino cultures and use them positively as assets, or other such issues. In other words, we need to get away from blaming the students for broad patterns like these. Also, if we are going to create equitable schools, we must recognize that these discipline disproportionalities undermine the achievement of that equity. Typically, when students are being disciplined, they are not sitting in a classroom learning, meaning that disproportionalities in discipline will directly translate into inequities in achievement. In other words, to have equitable schools, there must be equitable discipline.

A PROCESS FOR ADDRESSING INEQUITIES IDENTIFIED BY EQUITY AUDITS

Though we will not go through examples in any additional areas, there are plenty of other areas you can apply equity audits to. You can use them for addressing who is taking college track classes and who is not. For example, we studied a district in which few children of color and few children from low-income families were taking algebra during the year students needed it in order to be prepared for college. The district leadership studied their entire system and designed some changes to address this issue. As a result, the district has improved year by year the percentage of these children taking algebra in the right year for college prep and has improved the success of these children in algebra. Once again, it wasn't the kids; it was the adults who run the system and who can change the system that made the difference.

This example about algebra is a really important one. Indeed, it is not without reason that Robert Moses (Moses & Cobb, 2002), the well-known civil rights advocate, and others have begun to talk about learning algebra as a civil rights issue for students of color. Algebra taken the right year and then followed by the right series of math courses is extremely important if children of color and children from low-income families are going to have a good chance at attending and succeeding in college.

While in the past, educators have not systematically examined the inequities in the math literacy pathway (i.e., equity auditing), schools and districts working on becoming both equitable and excellent have begun to do so. The main thing that they have found is that educators can "engineer" a system that will yield more and more students of color and students from low-income families entering these courses in the right years and succeeding. For example, in the urban district we talked about earlier that has changed its system to increase equity in algebra achievement, the average scores on the state's algebra test, a difficult test, for African American students changed from abysmally low to higher than the average score for all students statewide. This is an example of using an equity audit to change the system internally to yield greater equity districtwide.

There is, thus, a simple process you too can use to address inequities in your school or district. We have summarized the steps in the following outline:

Step 1: Choose an area to examine and disaggregate your data, but do all of this collaboratively; involve teachers, administrators, parents, and other community members in this process.

Step 2: Analyze to figure out why the inequitable pattern is happening. What is causing it? Where does it start within the educational system? Do this collaboratively.

Step 3: Devise a possible solution. Do this collaboratively.

Step 4: Implement the solution.

Step 5: Monitor the results. If the solution works, celebrate. If it does not, return to Step 2 above and repeat the process.

Now, let's examine these steps more closely. First, pick an area to investigate. It is generally best to take on only one issue at a time. As we mentioned earlier, one of the problems with civil rights equity audits is that they identify so many areas that need work that people become overwhelmed about where to start. After you have picked the area to apply the equity audit, take some time and look at the numbers in this area for your school or district. Unless you have already achieved equity, you will find the same kind of disproportionate percentages that we've discussed in the preceding examples. This is powerful evidence of systemic patterns of inequities. Looking at your data to determine if you have these kinds of systemic patterns of inequity is best done either with selected staff or with all your staff. Your findings will likely sink in better if people participate together in the analysis of the data.

The second step is to analyze why the inequitable patterns happen. Where do they start? Elementary, middle, or high school? Why aren't LEP, Latino, African American, and low-income students being identified for GT classes? Do teachers and other staff need to reconsider their identification categories? Who does identification? What conscious and unconscious criteria are being used? The point is to ask questions, explore, find out how the inequity patterns are emerging.

The third step is to devise solutions based on your collaborative analyses of the data. You can go to the research literature, internal and external experts or scholars, or other schools and districts. The fourth step is to implement these solutions. The fifth is to rigorously monitor or evaluate these solutions, using your data. If you don't see improvements in the patterns of who gets into GT, you work collaboratively to figure out where the problem is, devise new solutions, and monitor and evaluate the results. Finally, when you do achieve success, celebrate. Achieving equity and excellence is critically important, so always celebrate when you move forward on this great journey.

Once you have completed this process, you need to follow a similar process on other possible areas of inequity. Some of these areas are the following:

- Attendance
- Drop outs
- Participation in extracurricular activities (including academic-focused areas, such as speech and debate, as well as athletics, art, music, etc.)
- Representation in student organizations, such as student government, cheerleading, pep squad, etc.
- Completion of advanced graduation plans vs. regular diplomas vs. GED completion
- Foreign language program enrollment
- Career/technology programs (both overrepresentation in traditional "hands-on" courses, such as auto mechanics, and underrepresentation in high-tech career training, such as the Microsoft or Cisco certification programs in place in some high schools)

We call the analysis of these areas taken together *programmatic equity auditing*. You are auditing the systemic patterns of equity or inequity in all of the different programs offered by your school or district. In all cases, you are using already collected data to identify and address internal patterns of inequity.

USING EQUITY AUDITS ON ACHIEVEMENT DATA AND TEACHER QUALITY DATA

We have two other areas that we include under our concept of equity audits. One is the accountability performance data itself. This means disaggregation—by race, income group (usually free- and reduced-lunch status is used to identify those from low-income families, even if this measure under-estimates those from these families), English-speaking status, and so forth—of your scores by subject and grade on your accountability tests, both the state's annual one and the internal ones the district has devised. While this was routinely done in only a few states in the past, the new *No Child Left Behind Act* requires this kind of disaggregation.

With these areas, you do the same as was described in the previous section. That is, you analyze where the inequities are, devise interventions, implement these, evaluate the intervention results, and repeat the process if steady progress is not evident. For example, you may find that African American and Latino students are not doing well in math throughout the school or district. To address this, you carefully analyze the data, devise a solution, implement it, monitor the results, and revise the solution if it is not working. If it is working, make a big deal out of it. Celebrate together; get people enthused that these inequities can be addressed and erased.

The third area we include in our equity audits is what we call *teacher quality equity*. Teacher quality usually means the years of experience and the level of education of the teacher. Though it is certainly easy to disagree over whether these are the best indicators of teacher quality, it is usually assumed that the more years of experience teachers have and the higher the level of their education, the better teachers they are, on average.

There is growing consensus among researchers and practitioners that teacher quality is the prime determinant of students' opportunities for academic success (Darling-Hammond & Sclan, 1996; Ingersoll, 1999; Prince, 2002). The state of Tennessee, in fact, has formalized this belief by including a "value added" component to its state accountability system that tracks, by teacher, the improvement of students on state standardized tests (see Sanders & Rivers, 1996). For this reason and others, some include teacher quality equity in a broader classification called "opportunity to learn" (OTL; see Banks et al., 2001).

If your district is considering teacher quality, equity requires that you examine the distribution of teacher quality throughout the schools in your district. Which schools have the highest and lowest percentage of the most experienced teachers? Unless the district has worked on this, you will find that the percentage of experienced teachers is highest in the schools with the most white middle-class students and that the highest percentage of least experienced teachers is at the schools serving predominantly children of color and children from low-income families. You will likely find the same patterns of inequity when assessing the number of teachers teaching outside their expertise area, teacher mobility, and teacher level of education.

You can do some similar work, though, just within your own school. Are your most experienced teachers, your most stable teachers, your teachers with the highest level of education, and your teachers teaching within their area of expertise teaching only the "best" students? On the other hand, is the opposite true? Are your least educated teachers, your most mobile teachers, your least experienced teachers, and your teachers teaching outside their area of expertise assigned to the lowest track students and/or more of the students of color or those from low-income families? If the answer to these questions is "yes," as is the case in many schools, then you have uncovered patterns of inequity that have to be addressed. How can we expect to do well with all students if we continue to provide the best, most experienced, most educated, most stable teachers to certain groups of students and continue to provide the opposite to other groups of students?

We know that some educators will protest that you can't do anything about which schools and courses teachers gravitate to, especially teachers with seniority. We have had this said to us many times when we raise this issue. However, this is just not true. First, there are schools and districts that have successfully addressed these issues and thus do not have these inequitable patterns in the distribution of teacher quality. Second, which teachers teach which kids is a matter of district or school policies. You can work your way through to policies that support and yield an equitable distribution of teacher quality, even in "union" states.

Consider, for example, how decisions are made about which teachers teach which students? Is seniority or political viability the real basis for the decisions, whatever the written policy and procedure might say? It is probably best to collaborate with the district's educators at all levels when working to address inequitable teacher distribution among different student groups. This may be difficult, but it is the approach that will be seen as having the greatest legitimacy by teachers. If we are serious about creating equitable schools, we must recognize that these inequitable distributions of teacher quality undermine the achievement of that equity. The way, then, to address this inequity is to use the same process as discussed above: Collaboratively analyze the data, collaboratively interpret the data, collaboratively design solutions, monitor the results, and celebrate success if successful or repeat the process if not.

We are not interested in owning, copyrighting, or controlling the use of equity audits as we have defined them here, so you can freely use them. Indeed, we strongly urge educators to use them. You can come up with other areas where you can apply the basic idea. You need to have data on an area. You need to analyze it for patterns of inequity. You need to devise solutions, implement them, evaluate the results, and cycle through again if improvement is not occurring. In addition, you need to celebrate when you succeed.

Another good resource that assists in using data to address inequities within the school is Ruth Johnson's (2002) *Using Data to Close the Achievement Gap: How to Measure Equity in Our Schools.* Some of you may have seen this in its earlier version, published by the Achievement Council and called *Setting Our Sights: Measuring Equity in School Change* (1996). Friends of ours told us about this resource after we had begun our work on equity audits, and we think it is excellent.

CONCLUSION

In public education, as in many other public areas, we are collecting more and more data and making the data available to more and more people. In our view, this is good for democracy. Schools are public institutions that should be transparently open to the public that pays for the services. In this chapter, we have illustrated how we can use the collected data to uncover inequities that are internal to the systems we run as educators. We have given examples of doing this with GT, special education, and discipline data, but the method can be applied in many other areas for which we have data. We have also discussed a simple process for using the data to change how we do things. Our experience is that people "get" equity audits quickly and easily. They could even be used with your school board and with parents. Especially if graphs are used, it is easy to see the problems uncovered by these audits when the results are illustrated in this way.

In the next chapter, we will focus specifically on school leadership. We will discuss some essential characteristics of leadership, ways to sustain yourself as a leader, ways to constantly improve leadership, and ways of working with assistant principals—all with a focus on developing schools that are equitable and excellent.

CHAPTER SEVEN

School Leadership and Continuous Improvement

> *We have our own bodies and spirits and the justice of our cause as our weapons.*
>
> *There are many reasons for why a man does what he does. To be himself he must be able to give it all. If a leader cannot give it all, he cannot expect his people to give anything.*
>
> —César Chávez (1968), leader for
> the civil and economic rights
> of U.S. agricultural workers

We all know that good leadership, the "bodies and spirits" of our leadership, is crucial to "the justice of our cause" for equity and excellence in schooling. In fact, many would say that strong, outstanding leadership is necessary to any significant transformation of any organization, schools included (Glickman, 2002). However, we all also know that one person's leadership does not carry the whole show.

Teachers and other staff, including counselors, instructional aides, librarians, nurses, school secretaries, custodians, and other support staff, often provide key leadership in a school. Some scholars (see Spillane, Halverson, & Diamond, 2001) refer to this concept as "distributed leadership." Thus, what we are interested in here is that *everyone* should think of herself or himself as simultaneously being a leader and being a follower, even the principal or superintendent. This chapter, then, is about leadership, and it is for everyone. We will discuss what leadership is in our view and, most important, what leadership for equitable and excellent schools entails.

THREE ESSENTIAL CHARACTERISTICS OF LEADERSHIP FOR EQUITY AND EXCELLENCE

The most important characteristic of a leader—whether a principal, teacher leader, counselor, or custodian—who is creating or who is going to create an equitable and excellent school is that this person has developed a strong ethical or moral core focused on equity and excellence as the only right choice for schools in a democracy. For this person, this is an indomitable belief, an indomitable commitment.

A leader for equity and excellence understands that the most important issue in public education is creating schools that are both equitable and excellent. This leader understands that it is our responsibility—our ethical and moral responsibility, even our sacred or spiritual responsibility—to create such schools. This leader understands that this responsibility is central to our country's long history of dedication to equity for all people—for working people, the poor, women, people of color, people with disabilities, for any people who have been excluded. This leader, whatever her or his position within the school, understands that this mission for equity and excellence in our nation's schools is part of a 200-year-old civil rights movement that is central to what is truly valuable about our country. (A good resource on this moral, or spiritual, dimension of leadership is the "Spirituality in Leadership" (2002) issue of *School Administrator*, containing articles by Paul Houston, Deepak Chopra, Michael Fullan, John Hoyle, and Margaret Wheatley, among others.)

This ethical, moral, and democratic core has to be kept strong within each of us. There will be constant forces, constant push and pull, to get, make, or force each of us to abandon this core. Even many powerful people, including superintendents, principals, school board members, professors in education, deans of colleges of education, university presidents, and others, will oppose your efforts to make this the core of your work. As we have discussed before, many at all levels within education truly do not believe that all children can learn. They have all kinds of reasons and defenses, and they will often try to get others to believe as they do. Also, many just do not understand equity and its critical importance. They will want to ignore it or relegate it to a back burner or even try to remove it altogether as a legitimate goal. They see protecting themselves, their biases against equity, or their territory as more important than working for equity and excellence. The simple truth is that for any of us to be a leader for equity and excellence, regardless of our position in our organization, requires that we maintain our commitment no matter what others around us do or say or believe.

In addition, learn not to be afraid of those above you. This is very important, but it is difficult for many Americans. Most of us grow up having been taught to be afraid of those above us in an organization. We are intimidated by their power, by their ability to control our future or fire us. Our experience has shown that we all have been taught to worry about this or to fear it too much, typically beyond what is realistic. We believe, from our own daily experiences, that there is much more space within our organizations to act *for* equity than we typically think. We think our internalized fear is often greater than the situation truly justifies, and because of this internalized fear, inequity is left to fester and grow.

We are not, though, suggesting that anyone needs to be rash or stupid. We also are not saying that anyone should go down in flames over every little issue. We need to always be thoughtful and careful. We need to pick our battles and when to make a stand. At the same time, we always need to be worrying about whether we are being judicious when we are really just protecting ourselves. It is a simple fact that just as maintaining democracy requires constant vigilance and constant bravery, so does not giving in to fear to work openly for equity.

Another key part of being able to act for equity is always being respectful to everyone, no matter whom. Even if a person is supporting inequity. Even if we strongly disagree with someone or are highly critical of someone's behavior, decisions, and so on, we can still treat that person with respect. We can even directly confront someone and be highly respectful at the same time. Indeed, we think we must always do this. Nothing in our view calls for disrespect, but acting for equity often means directly addressing issues that make others uncomfortable. However, there will typically be many fewer negative consequences if we treat everyone with respect, even though we may be raising issues that cause significant discomfort. In contrast, if we are disrespectful, we usually shut down any conversation or any possibility for positive change.

Again, for whatever reason, many people in this country grow up afraid of authority, afraid of those above us, afraid of their power over us, afraid of their power to fire or take out their revenge on us. We, too, have experienced this, but the best, most successful leaders struggle to rid themselves of this fear, and this is usually an ongoing struggle rather than a case of achieving complete success and then just enjoying it. However, when you do learn not to be afraid, you gain more freedom to act in ways that are more effective for yourself and for equity and excellence in your educational environment. You can learn to have your decisions and actions flow out of your values, out of your beliefs, rather than out of fear. When you do this, people around you, even those above you, over time, develop respect for you. Everyone comes to know that you consistently act out of your values. They know approximately where you will be on any issue, and they know that you won't falter or stumble or change your beliefs just because someone more powerful in the organization disagrees with you. This is especially true if you always treat everyone with great respect.

A second characteristic that leaders for equity and excellence have is a deeply held belief—a faith—that positive growth and improvement in both equity and excellence is truly possible. Many will say that improving equity is too idealistic, not realistic, not possible. This is simply not true. Every day there are educators who are moving equity and excellence forward in interactions with others, in a single classroom, in a single school, in a district, in a whole state. There are already literally thousands of educators who are already strongly committed to equity and excellence and to moving this forward.

Thus, pessimism or cynicism is just not allowed, at least not for very long. Of course, there are battles that you will lose. There are golden opportunities that fail. It does get really difficult and frustrating sometimes. However, if you maintain your core, your center, your commitment to equity and excellence, if you keep faith and keep working, you will also have battles that you win and opportunities that flourish. We have experienced this ourselves, and we have talked to many others who have had the same experience. We can act for equity, and we will have successes that we can deeply value and cherish; not just a few, either, but many.

A third characteristic of a leader for equity and excellence is that she or he never quits. She or he—you—never quits working for equity and excellence. You never quit pushing for it. You become what has been described as a "stubbornly persistent" leader in your insistence on working toward equity and excellence in your school (Riester et al., 2002). Indeed, you understand you never can quit. Students who are at the bottom, so far down they have very few real choices, only have us who make this commitment. They don't get to quit being at the bottom; they don't have this choice. Children don't get to choose to no longer experience inequity. For example, if there is racism toward children of color, they don't get to quit being children of color experiencing that racism. If you understand what equity is about and how critically important it is, if you have a core commitment to equity and excellence, if you believe that you can make a difference, you just don't get to quit. You do not allow yourself to quit. You understand that to quit is to betray the children who do not get the choice or the chance to quit. Instead, you are persistent, relentless, unstoppable in your continuing work to increase equity and excellence.

Sustaining Yourself as a Leader for Equity and Excellence

In the course of our work as professors and researchers, we interact constantly with graduate students, teachers, school administrators, policymakers, community members, parents, and other university faculty. Many of these people are also highly successful and influential leaders, and many of the ones we interact most with share our strong commitments to developing schools that are both equitable and excellent. Our conversations with these individuals and groups, both formal and informal, frequently focus on what it takes to do this kind of work—what is required to be a leader in a school working toward equity and excellence. It frequently comes up that this is incredibly difficult work and that leaders who engage in it must consciously strategize ways to make progress in almost impossible circumstances, and they must strategize ways to sustain themselves in the midst of such a challenging pursuit. In this section we share some of the suggestions and strategies either used by the leaders with whom we have worked or devised by ourselves.

1. You cannot do this work alone; you need allies who share your commitments and who are willing to work alongside of you. Part of your job as a leader is to develop allies on your own staff, but this is not the only place they can be

found. Look for allies in many different places. They are not always in your school. They may be in other schools, in other districts. They may be in other organizations in your community—in social work, law enforcement, health care, city and county government, businesses, charitable organizations, civic advocacy organizations, houses of worship, universities, professional organizations, and many other places. They may be individual parents. Wherever they are, whoever they are, team up, work together, support and sustain each other.

2. Your allies should be connected to one another as well as to you. In other words, build networks constantly. Build them inside your organization and outside your organization. Build them with parents and community people. Build them with other professional staff. Create networks, webs of people working for equity and excellence in education. Building multiple networks, formal and informal, helps build equity, helps increase the power of equity as a force in our educational system and in our society.

3. Try always to treat everyone with respect and appreciation as a human being, even the most difficult people who you encounter, even—especially—the people who attack you personally. Honor all people as fellow human beings. This is an area in which many of us think we do well, but where, in fact, deeper reflection might lead us to see that we need to improve. Treating people with respect means trying very hard to understand and dignify the perspective of people with whom you may have fundamental, strongly held disagreements. However, treating everyone with respect and appreciation does not mean not confronting people, not engaging with people on difficult issues. Treating everyone with respect and appreciation but not being willing to engage over difficult issues is superficial and can be perceived as being condescending. On the other hand, confronting and engaging with people over difficult issues without showing respect and appreciation is destructive and breeds hostility. Try hard to do neither. Instead, strike a balance in which you always show respect for others' viewpoints—but never shrink from expressing your own.

4. Constantly plant seeds of equity and excellence everywhere you go. Not all will bloom and flourish. Many seeds that you really liked will just not take hold, but keep planting anyway. When one starts to grow, support it, water it, help it flourish. These small seeds can be planted in any and every one of the hundreds of two-to-three-minute interactions you have with people every day, that is, the conversations over the copy machine, the minor decisions about student discipline, the greetings to parents picking up and dropping off children, the seemingly routine phone calls, the walk-throughs of teachers' classrooms, the assignments of teacher duty, and countless others. Let virtually every situation be an opportunity to seed, grow, or sustain equity.

5. If you are in a position of formal authority, try hard not to see yourself as the boss. Instead, see yourself as the facilitator. Don't try to do your work in an authoritarian fashion. If you lead in an authoritarian fashion, this just makes people do what you want because they have to. An authoritarian approach does not make people feel positive about change or have any ownership of it. In addition, as soon as the authority figure is gone or even gone from sight, people will revert because they don't really believe; they are just being obedient. However, we are not saying that leaders should be afraid of making decisions when necessary. Moreover, we know that it is always an ambiguous line that divides involving others in decision making from making decisions yourself. This is just part of the difficulty and complexity of being a good leader.

6. Have a vision of equity and excellence, and repeat it constantly; make it clear and straightforward so people can clearly understand it. For example, when one of us questioned a highly respected national educational leader about what kind of a speech he would recommend for talking to a group of parents about equity and excellence, he replied, "I only have one speech." This was his way of saying that he had a clear message that he repeated to everyone at every opportunity.

7. Lead as a servant. You are there to serve the children, their parents, your community, the other educators, and staff you work with. Most of the day-to-day work of leadership is really service to others.

8. Being a leader is not about enhancing your ego. So many, many leaders use their position to enhance their ego or use their position to enhance their power or to protect their space or territory—though they often say they don't. People can easily get corrupted by position and power. Moreover, this corruption is typically not blatant but subtle. If you have position or power, give it away constantly. Ask others to confront you if you are using your power or position to enhance your ego. While it is hard, always be open to anyone telling you this. When we asked one of the best principals we have ever studied—a principal who took a school dominated by children from low-income families who did not speak English and developed it into one of the finest schools we have ever seen—what was the most important thing a principal needed to learn, she said that the most important thing that any leader can do is lay aside his or her ego. This is definitely not easy, but definitely very important.

9. Learn not to fear or become defensive about criticism. Be open to it, and even seek it. There is almost always some truth in criticism, even when badly or disrespectfully conveyed. Create a personal and organizational climate in which everyone is interested in hearing and engaging with criticism. We have seen so many leaders who become intensely defensive at any criticism. Indeed, many try to take revenge at any criticisms, but there is nothing more destructive to an organization or a leader than to take revenge at those who criticize you. Although we know that this, too, is hard, learning to hear the truth in any criticism makes you a much more influential and more effective—a more transformational—leader. If you can master this skill, you can always be using criticism to improve what you are doing. We do not mean to say that you have to be perfect and never get defensive. Instead, we are saying to continually struggle to be open to criticism.

10. Honor commitments you make to others. These commitments can be large or small, but keeping them (to students, to teachers, to parents, to community members) is an important part of building trust. Furthermore, having the trust of the people who work with you is essential in doing the work that will be required to make your school a place where both equity and excellence are present.

Of course, no one is perfect about all of these all of the time, but we can always be working on them. That is what we are trying to do. We all make mistakes daily, but we can also pick ourselves up and try again, constantly struggling to build equity and excellence.

A NOTE FOR CAMPUS AND DISTRICT LEADERS ON BUILDING LEADRSHIP CAPACITY

Many have begun to understand that if a school or district is to improve the academic achievement of all children, all the teachers in a school or district must constantly be improving their abilities to be successful with all of the children in their classrooms. Many people think, though, that this means that just the weak and average teachers must improve. However, we have found that it is better to think that all teachers, no matter how weak or how strong, need to be constantly improving. Teaching is like art or writing; there is no ceiling. You can always get better. This is sometimes called "constantly building capacity," which means constantly improving the skills of all teachers to successfully teach all children.

What many people, though, do not realize is that the same is true for leadership. If a school or district is to continually improve its success with all of its children, all of the leadership—not just some, but all—must be on an increasing curve of improvement. Like art, writing, and teaching, there is no top end or ceiling to leadership. Any leader can always get better and better. This, too, is called constantly building capacity.

Those in district leadership positions, in particular, need to think about this with respect to all of the campus leadership.

What we have found is that it is not useful to think that just the weaker principals need improvement. Instead, it is best to think that if a district is to become an equitable and excellent district, all leadership must be constantly improving. Indeed, the very best districts have this quest for improvement as a central focus. They, in effect, have an ongoing program of professional development for all of their leadership, just as they do for the teachers and other staff.

A NOTE TO PRINCIPALS AND DISTRICT LEADERS ABOUT ASSISTANT PRINCIPALS

In your efforts to constantly improve leadership, don't leave out ongoing professional development for assistant principals. Many districts provide ongoing training for their principals, but ignore their assistant principals. APs are key members of the leadership team, and they are usually the main source of future principals and district leaders. They, too, need to be on a constant program of improvement.

What happens in many schools is that assistant principals end up with fairly narrow areas of responsibility that the principal is not interested in. Then, the assistant principals are left there throughout the school year, or even many years. Another model is to divide up the assistant principals among grades or areas of responsibility and then leave them in that area for years. Indeed, many principals seem to find it hard to think of assistant principals as their colleagues. Instead, many principals seem to think that assistant principals are just there to serve them. This is very unfortunate for the assistant principals and for the future of leadership in education.

What is really needed is for each principal to think about preparing her or his assistant principals to become principals who lead for equity and excellence. This means that each assistant principal needs to have experience in all areas of campus leadership. This means mentoring. This means the principal paying attention to the leadership development of the assistant principals throughout the year.

What we have found to be best for this leadership development is for the principal and assistant principals to work as a leadership team. This helps everyone to be on the same page. This helps everyone to know all areas of leadership. This builds trust. Each team member knows nearly the same as all team members, so each one will typically make nearly the same decision no matter what the situation. In addition, this teaming models what needs to happen with teachers and other staff. Indeed, the whole building needs to be teaming to create success, to create both equity and excellence.

CONCLUSION

In this chapter we have brought the focus more sharply to leadership for equity and excellence. We discussed three characteristics of such leadership: (1) an ethical, moral, and democratic core; (2) a deeply held belief or faith that we can create equitable and excellent schools; and (3) the commitment to never quit, to never allow ourselves that choice, because the children experiencing inequity never get to choose to quit. We also provided ten strategies that we think can help you sustain yourself as a leader. Many of these we understand are hard to implement, and we typically never employ any of them perfectly. Nonetheless, we can still always bring ourselves back to them. We also commented briefly on the fact that there needs to be a district commitment to improve the leadership capacity of *all* school leaders, from the best to the weakest. We suggested that, just as in teaching, there is no limit to how good you can get. We ended with a plea for principals to work with assistant principals differently. We recommended that assistant principals be seen as equal members of the leadership team and that they not be relegated to single areas, but rather become involved in the broad work of the school.

In the next chapter, which is a short one, we discuss what we call *proactive redundancy*, a phenomenon we "discovered" in schools and districts seriously working on achieving equity and excellence. We define the phenomenon and show how it can be applied in numerous areas of schooling.

CHAPTER EIGHT

Proactive Redundancy

> *Greatness does not come to any people on flowery beds of ease. We must fight to win the prize. No people to whom liberty is given, can hold it as firmly and wear it as grandly as those who wrench their liberty from the iron hand of the tyrant. The hardships and dangers involved in the struggle give strength and toughness to the character, and enable it to stand firm in storm as well as in sunshine.*
>
> —Frederick Douglass (1881), former
> slave, author, and statesman

While Frederick Douglass's choice of words may differ from that of contemporary writers, his point is our point. Equity and excellence does not come to us on "flowery beds of ease. We must fight to win the prize." Furthermore, what we do to achieve equity and excellence *does* "give strength and toughness to the character, and enable it to stand firm in storm as well as in sunshine." In this chapter, we describe a phenomenon we found in whole districts that are successfully improving the learning of their diverse students (see Skrla et al., 2000), and we believe learning the lessons of this phenomenon—which gave "strength and toughness . . . to stand firm in storm as well as in sunshine"—will help us "win the prize" of equity.

The fact that the concept we call *proactive redundancy*, which we will define shortly, comes from a research project about successful districts—as opposed to individual campuses—is significant. One of the goals of this particular research project was to gain an understanding of the conditions in districts that made it possible for multiple campuses to achieve high levels of academic success with large populations of children from low-income homes. In contrast, most earlier success stories in the research literature focused on single schools, and these schools were often regarded as "miracles" or "mavericks."

What we found in the four districts we focused on in our research (Skrla et al., 2000) was a district culture in which the failure of children—any children—to learn was unacceptable. In order to prevent this unacceptable failure from happening (as opposed to "fixing" it once it had occurred), these districts created multiple, overlapping processes to ensure that all students learned. It was the creation of these multiple, overlapping, "redundant" processes that we termed proactive redundancy.

This terminology was adapted from the structure of organizations, like nuclear power plants, that simply cannot allow failure. These plants, for instance, have multiple backup processes or systems so that if one process or system fails, there is another to take its place. Thus, *proactive* means that these multiple backup processes or systems were planned and built into the system ahead of time. *Redundancy*, then, means that there are two or more processes or systems focused on one goal. The cost of system failure would be so high—the failure of students, in our case—that multiple systems are built in to perform the same functions in case the primary system or the first backup system fails.

This same idea was at work in the successful districts we studied. It is an idea, or philosophy, that needs to be in place in all schools and districts committed to equity and excellence for all children. We cannot afford to have some children or some groups of children not learning. Consequently, we need to plan and develop ahead of time multiple processes or systems to ensure that all children are learning. In the districts we studied, this approach to ensuring that all students are learning can be found both at a single level of the school organization (such as within a classroom) and on different levels of the school organization, such as within the classroom, the campus leadership, and the central office.

Proactive Redundancy in the Classroom

Our first illustration of proactive redundancy is a single-level example from the classroom. If a teacher plans and uses her or his voice, blackboard drawings, and manipulable models in the same lesson to show students how to do some skill, that is proactive redundancy. It is proactive because the use of more than one modality of teaching (to reach more than one learning style) is planned ahead of time. It is not remediative (i.e., done after the fact to compensate for a lack of learning); it is proactive. It is redundant because more than one way to learn is being provided.

Likewise, still at the level of the classroom, teachers commonly plan multiple lessons ahead of time that are focused on the same content, knowing that more than one lesson taught in more than one way will be required for all students to grasp the content being taught. The difference between these practices, which are now fairly common among teachers, and what was at work in our successful districts, however, was perhaps most striking in the expectations for the outcomes of teacher practices. The teachers in these districts assessed student progress frequently through a variety of formal and informal assessments, and the expectation was clear: All students were expected to master whatever was being taught. If these assessments showed that some students needed additional or different instruction to grasp the concept, the students received it immediately (through a variety of flexible instructional arrangements, including flexible grouping within the classroom, exchanging students with other team or grade-level teachers, tutorial periods, after-school tutoring, and Saturday school).

PROACTIVE REDUNDANCY IN TEACHER PROFESSIONAL DEVELOPMENT

A second example of proactive redundancy at work is a multi-level example—a principal helping a teacher to improve his or her teaching. In this effort, the principal plans two or more ways to assist this teacher. The principal may visit the teacher weekly to provide assistance and then may communicate some helpful ideas. The principal may also arrange to send the teacher to professional development that directly relates to the teacher's area in need of improvement. Third, the principal may arrange a substitute so that the teacher can spend time observing and interacting with a master teacher.

The idea here is that the principal is working in multiple ways to build the teacher's capacity to be successful with the children in her or his classroom. While, typically, teachers in need of assistance do not receive the help they need to improve until after an entire year (or many entire years) has passed and many children have suffered the consequences, proactive redundancy means planning *and executing* more than one way to improve this teacher's work. It means using two or more ways to increase the possibility that the teacher will actually improve. An example of this can be seen in the following description by a principal from one of our study districts of his teacher supervision process:

> I'll meet with my teachers five or six times throughout the year just to see, individually with them, how they're doing with their students. And I basically ask them, "What's your plan to do this?" And they'll give me their plans. And then throughout the year, at least once in each six weeks we'll sit down, and we'll meet and I'll say,

"How are your students progressing? Do you need extra help? Do I need to assign somebody to help you?" And we have the instructional coaches that work in the central office area that come in and help the teachers.

This process utilizes proactive and redundant methods to ensure that teachers are doing what is needed to make certain that all students are reaching achievement standards.

Proactive Redundancy Involving District Support Staff

A third example is a multilevel one involving district staff, principals, and classroom teachers. This example is from one of the best districts we have seen, an urban district with over 90% of its students children of color and a similar percentage of children from low-income homes. In this district, the district leadership worked very closely with each principal to ensure that the quality of leadership, especially as that leadership focused on student learning, was constantly good and constantly getting better. Much of this effort to ensure high-quality leadership was undertaken by area superintendents who were responsible for ongoing leadership capacity building in their areas.

However, the district leadership also had district-level curriculum and instruction experts assisting teachers throughout the district, based on the specific needs of a teacher or a group of teachers. The district leadership met with each one of these experts on a monthly basis to get their input about the schools they visited. Consequently, while the district leadership put great stock in their principals and area superintendents and worked with them to ensure their success (their success meaning that the children in their schools were succeeding academically), this district leadership also had another presence on campuses via the curriculum and instruction specialists. This, too, then, was proactive redundancy. The district leadership did not rely only on the pathway through principals or only on their area superintendents to provide needed assistance and support for teachers; the leadership, in addition, established another route, through the instructional specialists, to build teachers' capacity to successfully teach all their students, and they monitored the progress of the teachers through all of these routes. In other words, the district leadership in this case had proactively developed three different ways (redundancy) to ensure teachers were succeeding.

THE IMPORTANCE OF PROACTIVE REDUNDANCY IN EQUITABLE AND EXCELLENT SCHOOLS

This concept of proactive redundancy may seem of obvious or minor importance given the enormity of the task of creating equitable and excellent schools. In our experience, however, it is central to both the philosophy and the practice in places where literally all children are learning at high levels. Our colleague, Joseph Johnson, who collaborated with us on the research about the successful districts that we've described in this chapter, talks frequently about the contrast between schools that believe in proactive redundancy and other schools that believe in what he calls the "Las Vegas approach to school improvement." By this he means that this second group of schools hire what they hope are good teachers and principals and then do little else except pull the handle on the achievement slot machine (annual achievement tests) once a year and hope fervently that they've "won."

In contrast, schools that practice proactive redundancy do not believe in gambling with children's futures. They leave as little as possible to chance and instead proactively build in as many supports and check points as possible to ensure that all children learn.

CONCLUSION

This has been a brief but important chapter. We could have included it in other chapters, but we thought it needed to be singled out because of its importance. All we did here was explain proactive redundancy and provide examples at all levels. The goal of proactive redundancy is to provide multiple processes—not just one—to ensure that all children are learning the material in the curriculum. We recommend this process because the districts we studied that were making substantial improvements in the education of children of color and children from low-income families had come up with this methodology. They hadn't created it consciously; the process just emerged from their efforts to be successful with all children. They didn't call it proactive redundancy; they didn't even have a specific name for doing this. They just did it. Our research team came up with the label after we had identified the phenomena. No matter who named it, though, we think it is an important process to see, understand, and replicate. The creators of the process were the district personnel, and it is the educators in these pioneer districts who should be valued for developing this approach to success for all students.

In the next chapter, we discuss parents, community, and context in relation to creating schools of equity and excellence. We strongly advocate for a different kind of parent and community involvement than is currently dominant. We argue for a deep, ongoing interweaving of the community and its schools. We also argue for schools learning to work with parents and community in ways that fit the needs and lives of the parents and the community—rather than expecting parents and community to fit the needs of schools. One important payoff from this approach is that it proactively decreases distance and alienation between schools and all of the communities that they serve.

CHAPTER NINE

Deep Collaboration With Parents and Community

While the battle for education in the early part of the century was fought in the courts, the battle for quality must be simultaneously waged in communities across the nation with real people and alliances. We know what works: equitable resources, smaller classes, quality teachers, and strong parental involvement [emphasis added].

—John H. Jackson, n.d., NAACP
national director of education

U nfortunately, the mainstream style of schooling has been one in which most schools have separated themselves from parents and community, that is to say, from their contexts. Of course, many educators would argue that their own schools have not done so. However, what we mean by a school being deeply connected to its students' parents and to its community is much different from what most schools consider the appropriate connection. What we mean is parents and other community members substantially involved in all aspects of schooling, from teaching and curriculum to discipline and organizational structure. We mean a deep interweaving of parents and community with the school and the school with the parents and the community.

Some scholars have suggested that the current separation originated in the past for specific reasons. They argue that it originated in an era when politicians and other powerful people controlled the schools and often used them primarily to employ relatives and associates rather than to educate children, though we have seen that this still exists in some small districts.

There was then a movement to professionalize the education system by taking control of the schools away from such people. The purpose of this was to make the primary focus of schools the education of children. While there may be some accuracy in this argument, it is likely that the issue is larger than this, since the professionalization of education parallels the professionalization of society in general. Nonetheless, whatever the historical reasons for separating schools from their parents and communities, it is no longer useful and can even be argued to be harmful.

Mostly what we have seen recommended in this area is a steady stream of advice about parent involvement and its importance to student success. Indeed, virtually everyone agrees that parent involvement is highly important. The problem with much of the research literature on this issue and with much of the parent involvement that commentators cite is that it involves a "model" of parent involvement that is most typical of white middle-class parents (Lopez et al., 2001).

From the educators' point of view, the "good" parent in this model attends regular parent group meetings; volunteers to help raise money for, or helps carry out, school activities; goes to school sports events; and shows up at theater productions, awards ceremonies, and so on. This good parent also responds quickly to any contacts from the school about problems with her or his child, supports the school's discipline of the child, treats the teachers or administrators with respect and deference, and, possibly, adds his or her own punishment to that required by the school. In fact, it is usually assumed that good parents have good children who do not typically get into any trouble at school.

Of course, all educators know that even the children of "good parents" get into trouble sometimes. Indeed, all educators know that this description is more the ideal than the reality, but, still, we think this is a pretty good, if brief, description of how educators would typically prefer parents to be.

There are, though, two main problems with this idea of good parents. First, it reinforces the notion that the school is primary and that parents need to mold themselves to what the school wants. Second, it, even if unconsciously, assumes a white middle-class cultural model that does not fit many of our schools' children, their parents, their communities, or their contexts. (We know that many white middle-class people do not think that they have a distinct culture, that only people of color have distinct cultures, but, actually, all people everywhere have a culture, and there clearly is one that is white and middle class. It is the one that is so prominent and dominant that it becomes invisible to many people.)

Let's examine the problems with the stereotypical views about good parents in the order we stated them. First, let's consider the problem of viewing the school as primary and the parents as secondary. When educators typically think about parents, we most often do not see them as partners, equal partners, who have as much say about what education should look like as do educators. The dominant assumption has been "Just give us your children." What we most often, deep down, mean by this is give us children who have been taught to be obedient to authority, give us children who are on grade level and ready to learn, give us children whose first language is English, give us children whose parents make them do all their homework, give us parents who have the knowledge to help their children when they do not understand a homework assignment, give us children who are well fed and well clothed, give us children who are positive and balanced. If you give us children who are all of these, then we will successfully educate them for college and for life.

In other words, the good parent does all those things that prepare the child to be ready to be taught. In this model, thus, the parent serves the educational system because, in the view of educators, this is what will work best if the child is to be successful in schools as they are typically designed (see Deschenes, Cuban, & Tyack, 2001).

We all know, of course, that it is much more complicated than this. We know that no matter what the differences may be between students and educators regarding level of family wealth, race, culture, or any other demographic factor, children, parents, and teachers are much more complex than this picture we have created. Even most of us would not fit this idealized view of what it means to be good parents. We know that there are problem kids at all schools; we know that there are problem parents at all schools; and we even know that there are problem teachers at all schools.

However, the important point here is that this typical, idealized picture that educators have of what good parenting is drives our attitudes and our behaviors toward parents and their involvement in our schools. Our dominant model is one in which parents are supposed to properly prepare students for us to work with, and the better that parents do this job, the higher the chances that we will be successful with their children.

What we want to suggest, as many others have, is that we need to rethink this model for all schools—for all parents. What we suggest is that educators and parents start thinking of schools as a real collaboration in which both educators and parents work together as *equal* partners to be successful with all children—with every unique, precious child.

The typical parent involvement model, as followed in most schools and districts, is thus a very limited model of parent involvement. What we are advocating is a much more substantial collaboration, a much more equal partnership. What we are advocating is that educators and parents collaborate on all facets of education. For example, we are suggesting that those parents who are available during the school day actually spend time in the classroom as coteachers, as partners in classroom education. We are suggesting that schools work to schedule significant activities during the weekend so that those parents who are only available on the weekend can become equal partners in the schooling of their children. We are suggesting that parents, as much as they are available, be involved in all aspects of schooling, including teaching, development of curriculum, enforcement of discipline, administration, and so forth. We are suggesting that schools figure out how to mold to the availability and interests of parents in order to bring them into a partnership. Indeed, in many ways, it would be helpful for us to think of ourselves as serving parents, rather than thinking of parents as serving or adjusting to us. Quite simply, a full and completely equal partnership is the best model, in our view.

We are especially suggesting, for instance, that educators help parents understand what the learning standards are that apply to all students and how children will be tested on these standards. We are suggesting that teachers literally sit down with their students' parents and go through the learning standards for their children. We are also suggesting that teachers sit down with the parents of their children and take the state test together. In all areas, teachers should always be helping parents understand exactly what is going on today with the schooling of their children. We know of schools that have done these things, and, when they are done well, they almost inevitably improve the achievement of children and the understanding that parents have of schooling in a standards-based era.

We would also suggest that educators expand this understanding of standards and accountability tests to include the whole community. For example, let's take a school within a sizeable city. Let's say it is an elementary school. Let's say there is an area of the community where the local people go to shop. Let's say this area has several small businesses and a large grocery store. What if, then, every week the school and the community put up a poster that the kids created, which helps everyone to understand one area of the standards or one area of the accountability test. What if each week the grocery store hands to each customer as she or he checks out a brief statement helping community members, parents, and students to understand one area of the standards. This could be coordinated with what children are learning that week. It could also be coordinated with an area the children are having trouble learning. This, then, is just one idea of a way in which the whole community takes ownership for what the children are learning and what they need to learn. It is one more facet of what we are recommending: a deep, comprehensive, persistent partnership between parents and educators to ensure both equity and excellence.

The second point we want to make is that when we think about parental involvement, unconsciously we use a model that fits white middle-class parents. In fact, we often unconsciously take it as *the* model, without even realizing it is a model. Then, when our parents do not fit this (unconscious?) model, we often automatically assume that these parents don't really care about their children. This is really a major problem. This negative or deficit-oriented assumption has major destructive effects. In fact, we typically do not even know our parents that well—have never been to their houses, have never talked with them about themselves and their lives in a positive way, have never developed meaningful relationships with them.

As a result, one of the most important changes to our assumptions that we need to make is to begin to understand that virtually all parents care deeply about their children. However, because of their cultures, their lifestyles, the difficulties in their lives, the limitations resulting from poverty, or other factors, our parents may express this caring in ways different from what educators are used to or expect (Young, 1998). Both of us have had long careers in education, and we can truly say that we have almost never met parents who did not care about their children. We have both also had many, many conversations with those who are not white or middle class. We have, though, met many parents whose caring was expressed in ways that were not well matched with the school's expectations or that made school personnel uncomfortable.

The most important thing that we can do, then, is to assume all parents really care—an assets approach that we have discussed in earlier chapters. We need to work to understand how this caring works for our parents. Instead of assuming that there is one correct approach to parent involvement, we need to develop parental involvement that fits the needs of the specific people in our community.

We can illustrate this with an example. We have a friend, Dr. Encarnacion "Chon" Garza, who is now a superintendent and has been a principal in two different schools. When he was a principal in his first school, he had many parents who lived in what are called *colonias*. Colonias are found in areas all along the border between the United States and Mexico. The colonias in which the parents of children in Chon's school lived were in the Rio Grande Valley area of Texas and were small parcels of land that had been sold to Mexican Americans who had very little income. These colonias, however, were a start for the people who inhabited them. They had become owners of their own property, though they were typically still making payments, just like most of the rest of us are. These small parcels often have no water, sewage, or electrical facilities. Also, there are typically no housing codes of any kind, so what people live in is often very rudimentary.

Chon's problem was that many of the parents in his school who lived in the colonias did not come to any school meetings. Chon's response, rather than to say that these parents didn't care, was to walk door to door in the colonias and meet and talk directly to these parents. He wanted the parents to see that he was someone who cared about and respected them, who wanted and needed their involvement with him in their children's education, so he went to see them in the environments that were most comfortable for them. Most important, though, he wanted these parents to see that he was someone they could trust.

The next thing Chon did was set up meetings of parents in the colonias. He got some parents to host the meeting in their yard. He invited the other parents to come not to the school but to the house or yard of one of their neighbor's to talk about their children's schooling. After he did this for some time, these same parents began coming to meetings at the school. Indeed, they became strong advocates for Chon, for his work to educate their children, and for their school.

Similarly, educators need to think about our specific parents—not some idealized parents, but the actual parents we have. We need to think creatively about how we can work with, fit, and mold to the culture, ways of living, and time schedules of the parents of the children in our schools.

If we need to conduct all meetings in two (or more) languages, we arrange that. If we need to meet in places and times that fit our parents' lives, we arrange that. We need to meet, come to know, and learn how to work with our parents in terms of who they are, rather than just require or expect parents to come to us and work with us in a manner that fits our educator ways.

In other words, we need to figure out how to have a real collaboration, a real partnership, with our parents—a partnership that works with who our parents are and with the way their lives work. We do not need to think of our parents, no matter who they are, in a deficit or negative way; we need to think of them in terms of their assets and the ways we can build positively on their assets. Thus, if many of our parents are Mexican American, we need to build positively on the culture, lives, and ways of these parents. If many of our parents are African American, we need to build positively on the culture, lives, and ways of these parents. If we have a diverse school, we build positively on all of that diversity.

Part of the problem for educators is that we often have biases (conscious or unconscious) about particular groups of people or particular cultures or neighborhoods. However, to approach any parent, culture, or neighborhood with the idea that our own ways are the correct ways is to doom our work on parent involvement. Think about how you want to be approached. You want people to approach you with a positive valuing of you. All parents want the same. This is very simple and very well known: Do unto others as you would want them to do unto you. We all, just like the parents of our children, want to be approached as if we have important assets to contribute. None of us want to be approached with the attitude that something is wrong with or lacking in us. Instead, just as we want for ourselves, we need to approach our parents with an assets attitude, with the attitude that every one of our parents is valuable, that every one of them has something important to contribute, and that we are committed to understanding and positively building on those assets.

One important way to do this is to connect to the history of the community and the history of the parents in our community. For instance, we know of one district that got their high school students working on collecting oral histories of their community and oral histories of the individuals in their community. This project was directly and consciously based on an assets approach. The project, thus, assumed that everyone had a valuable story to tell and that everyone—the parents, the students, the whole community—would benefit from learning individuals' and the community's histories.

One of the things that emerged in this oral history project was that some individuals who had before just seemed like ordinary community members who were usually ignored in the community turned out to be war heroes in World War II. Other community members had led very interesting lives, even though few people knew about this beforehand. When any of us learn the complex path that another's life has taken, we develop a deeper respect and appreciation for that person. Thus, this school project was based on building more positive, deeper relationships with the members of the community and was dedicated to doing this on an assets basis. It also deepened and improved the relationships between the school and the community and among all members of the community. Although initiated by the school, this project became a communitywide project and actually strengthened the whole community. This, then, is an exemplar of the kind of involvement with parents and community that we are recommending. (If you want more information on this particular effort, see the Llano Grande Center for Research and Development Web site at www.llanogrande.org.)

One issue that is important here is building positive relationships with one's community and all of its organizations. We recommend that you think of all of your community as your partners in education and that you integrate with all of them on the deepest level possible. For example, don't think of businesses just as sources of financial support or contributions of products; think about what the people in these businesses know that they can contribute. Do they use math in their jobs? If so, invite them in to help you teach math to your students. Are some of them writers of poetry, short stories, or other literary genres? If so, invite them in to teach your students. Do some of them have special knowledge in some area—sculpture, rock collecting, animals, flowers, or some other interesting field? If so, invite them in to help teach your students. Figure out ways that you can integrate them into all aspects of schooling.

The same is true for churches, mosques, synagogues, temples, or other houses of worship. Many of those attending religious services want to perform service of all sorts. Meet with them to see what they would like to contribute. Many of them have special skills, have had experiences during a war or the civil rights movement, or were part of major migrations of the U.S. population. Please note that we mean here houses of worship of all kinds—fundamentalist ones, liberal ones, small ones, Muslim, Buddhist, Jewish, and so on. Work with all of them; they are all part of your community. Some of the church members are retired teachers who would like to come back and help teach in some areas. Some churches might love to have the school choir perform for them or have the church choir perform for the school, giving both your students and the church members an opportunity for a public performance. Think creatively. Think how you can be full partners with all of your community. Make your school a cherished, beloved part of the community, a source of caring interactions, loving commitments, and treasured experiences.

One group of organizations that many educators do not think about is what we call advocacy or civil rights groups. We mean groups like the NAACP (National Association for the Advancement of Colored People), MALDEF (Mexican American Legal Defense and Education Fund), LULAC (League of United Latin American Citizens), and AARP (American Association for Retired People), among other similar organizations. Many of these groups feel excluded from schools but would love to be involved, would love to contribute. For example, members of the NAACP could come and talk about their participation in the civil rights movement. Some of them played key roles in changing your community's values. Members of the AARP could come and talk about the issues that the elderly in the community face. Many of these groups are very service oriented and would quickly work with your school and district if asked. In addition, if you are getting to know people in these organizations and working with them, you have decreased the chance that they will feel alienated from your school or district. Indeed, the best way to prevent conflict with any group is to work with them proactively to help you be successful with all students.

Take this same approach with the media. People working on newspapers, radio, and television have important skills that can be used to help you educate your community's children. Take your students to visit their work sites. Invite the media in to talk with your students about what they do. Ask them to help you get your students to understand how the media works. Ask them to help you plan class lessons in which they can make important contributions. See if your kids can't work with them and actually be on the radio or TV or in the newspaper. Have the media help you teach communication skills to your students.

We would also recommend that you work proactively with the political leadership in your community. Ask them to come and talk about being a legislator, a city council person, or a mayor. Ask them to work with you in designing lessons about legislatures and city politics. Ask them to come to your classes where your students can ask them questions. An additional benefit from these relationships is that they promote positive, constructive relationships between your school or district and the political leadership of your community. This means that you will probably prevent many of the misunderstandings that often occur between educational leaders in a community and its political leadership.

CONCLUSION

As you can see, we are talking about schools moving away from being so insular. We are talking about real partnerships with parents—partnerships that are molded in positive ways to fit the parents of your students, partnerships that are based on an assets approach rather than a deficit approach. We are also talking about building deep, comprehensive, ongoing partnerships with businesses, churches, advocacy and civil rights groups, the media, and the community's political leadership— literally all of the groups that are part of your community. Many, many people in your community would love to help, would love to contribute by helping educate the community's children. We are talking about thinking about schools and districts as deeply interwoven with all aspects of your community. We are talking about getting everyone, every organization in the community deeply involved with educating your school or district's children. We are talking about there being virtually no separation between the school, on one hand, and the parents and community, on the other.

Our final point is that if you have taken this book seriously, we should be saying directly to ourselves, to our parents, to all of our community, that we *all* should hold ourselves accountable for creating classrooms, schools, and districts that are both equitable and excellent. We all together need to expect nothing less than this. If we are not doing this, someone needs to point it out, to say it loudly, to shout it from the highest place.

From our experience in studying classrooms, schools, and districts that are highly successful with all students, regardless of student differences, we know it can be done. We know there is no legitimate excuse for not doing it. If we are not achieving this dream, someone needs to speak up. Someone needs to demand that *all* of us together—educators, parents, community members—put our hands to the sacred plow of education, that *all* of us, working together, push hard until we can all stand back and celebrate our successes, celebrate our great work together, celebrate accomplishing something that becomes a beacon to all of our people. We can, then, stand together and say that *we together* created equitable and excellent schooling for *all* of our children, every one of them.

The next chapter is the final one. In it, we review what this book has been about. We discuss what we see in the future, especially regarding the *No Child Left Behind Act of 2001*. Then, we end with our final call.

CHAPTER TEN

The Final Call

Working on the Dream
Each Day in Every Way

> *There's no turning back ... We will win. We are winning*
> *because ours is a revolution of mind and heart.*
>
> —César Chávez (1995)

> *A true revolution of values will soon cause us to question the*
> *fairness and justice of many of our past and present policies.*
> *On the one hand we are called to play the Good Samaritan on*
> *life's roadside, but that will be only an initial act. One day we*
> *must come to see that the whole Jericho Road must be trans-*
> *formed so that men and women will not be constantly beaten*
> *and robbed as they make the journey on life's highway. True*
> *compassion is more than flinging a coin to a beggar. It comes to*
> *see that an edifice which produces beggars needs restructuring.*
>
> —Martin Luther King, Jr. (1967)

This book is our call to all educators to become leaders for equity and excellence. It is our challenge to all of us, including ourselves.

We believe the time is ripe to move much, much closer in public education to attaining the "dream." We believe that this is truly possible in our own time.

All of the old deficit thinking about children that does not permit us to create classrooms, schools, and districts that are both equitable and excellent is wrong. Individually and collectively, we need to throw this deficit thinking away, banish it to the garbage heap of history.

Instead, we need to take on the challenge, the opportunity, to make sure, thoughtful, significant steps toward equity and excellence. We need to decide that we can figure this out. We need to make the commitment and then accept no excuses.

Every day, in things small and large, those of us who are educators are civil rights workers. We are on the frontlines every day. This civil rights work is our ordinary daily work. It is we who can make the education dream of both equity *and* excellence come true.

This is a journey, our journey, an American journey. This is a journey of education, but also a journey of the heart and mind, a journey of the spirit.

We are not the first, and we will not be the last on this great and courageous journey, but we are critically important at this critically important moment in history. We truly believe that there is in this historical moment—right now—the possibility for us to take some giant steps toward equity in education.

What We See in the Future

First, the *No Child Left Behind Act of 2001* (NCLB) has been enacted. For the first time in the history of U.S. education, the federal government has codified into law the position that achievement gaps between white children and children of color, between middle-class children and those from low-income homes are unacceptable and that schools and districts will be held accountable for closing these gaps:

> The NCLB Act will . . . [require] States to implement statewide accountability systems covering all public schools and students. These systems must be based on challenging State standards in reading and mathematics,

annual testing for all students in grades 3-8, and annual statewide progress objectives ensuring that all groups of students reach proficiency within 12 years. Assessment results and State progress objectives must be broken out by poverty, race, ethnicity, disability, and limited English proficiency to ensure that no group is left behind. School districts and schools that fail to make adequate yearly progress (AYP) toward statewide proficiency goals will, over time, be subject to improvement, corrective action, and restructuring measures aimed at getting them back on course to meet State standards. (U.S. Department of Education, 2002, ¶ 4)

We know that many people are criticizing language such as that above as mere rhetoric. We know that many educators think those in Washington do not know our reality or do not know what we really face. We (and others engaged in the work of equity) disagree. In fact, Wendy Puriefoy, president of the Public Education Network (a national organization of local education funds committed to advancing educational equity in low-income communities; see www.publiceducation.org), has said that the passage of NCLB is as significant as the 1954 *Brown v. Board of Education of Topeka* U.S. Supreme Court decision that resulted in school desegregation. While we can't say that we think NCLB is equal to the Brown decision, we do agree that even as rhetoric, it is a very important step. Even if it is only rhetoric to some of the powerful, once equity is rhetorically stated, just as racial or gender equity has been rhetorically stated, it becomes a legitimated standard that the nation can be called on to live up to.

Thus, we agree that codifying into national law that the achievement gap is unacceptable is highly important and historically significant. Certainly, it is true that some individuals and groups support this law for rhetoric-only purposes, but we would rather have this kind of inclusive rhetoric than a rhetoric that ignores all the children we have been leaving behind. Sure, there is much that Washington does not understand about schools. However, there are hundreds of people involved in the process of a major law like this, and many of them do understand what schools are like in all different kinds of circumstances. In addition, this law is not just a Republican law; it is a law made up of hundreds of compromises across the two parties and among groups and individuals within the parties, who, in turn, were without a doubt subject to considerable ongoing influence from outside groups.

Indeed, this law is a product of democracy, all the give and take, all the compromises. This means, in our view, that we should not treat this law simplistically; it is not a simple law. It is simply true that this law addresses a whole range of complex phenomena, some of which can be positive and some of which can be negative. We need to focus on what we can build, use, appropriate, and reframe to serve children. Of course, critique is very important (obviously we practice it ourselves), and it will always be, but if that is all we focus on, our question is whether this is the best we can do for all of our children. Consequently, it is not useful at all to simply disparage this law or to simply portray it as the work of the Bush administration.

In fact, this law takes some important steps in the directions we have advocated here, like disaggregation of accountability data by race and income groups. It also takes some steps that we disagree with, such as providing guaranteed school access to groups that have discriminatory policies. Nonetheless, as we recommended with standards and accountability, we need to find positive, constructive ways to work with this law to move equity forward. We strongly believe this can be done.

Second, as is apparent in this new law, standards and accountability are becoming more prominent and more important rather than becoming less important or fading from view. We know some critics will just increase the intensity of their reactions. However, again, we counsel finding constructive ways to appropriate or use standards and accountability to move equity forward. We know this is happening in many schools and districts and, thus, can happen in many more.

Third, if you are in a state just starting high-stakes testing with disaggregation by race and income group, the focus on achievement gaps will increase. Our experience is that many community groups, especially those supporting children of color, will become incensed at the differences in the achievement between their children and white middle-class children. This anger at the community's achievement gaps has always been there, but it will become more intense as achievement results are published. There will be anger and defensiveness, there will be conflict and conversation, but our experience is that much good can come out of this. Indeed, in every one of the districts we studied that have become much more successful with diverse children (and this is a finding we have seen no one else write about), the anger of community groups was a key catalyst to positive change in the district (Skrla et al., 2000).

Fourth, with these disaggregated high-stakes tests, educators in schools and districts will cheat. However, as instances of cheating are revealed by the media, your state agency should see how it can tighten the controls on this, such as requiring that a certain percentage of students—for instance, 95%—be tested. Some of the ways that people have already cheated have been assigning students to special education, overusing exemptions for limited English proficiency, finding ways to exclude students from testing (such as just telling them to not come to school the days of the tests or instituting restrictive discipline policies that allow suspension of certain students for minor offenses the day before testing), giving test answers to kids, or guiding them too much.

However, you can be ready for this. You can help the media be ready for it. You can examine data and help see that this cheating gets reported publicly, and you can work with your state education agency to devise solutions that prevent cheating from happening. It is virtually inevitable that cheating will occur, but you can use the experience of states like Texas that have gone through this to prepare to react quickly, to make sure that instances of cheating are revealed to the public, and to develop solutions that make cheating much more difficult.

Fifth, really focused work needs to be done on vetting high-stakes tests for obvious cultural biases, conscious or unconscious. Some will say that testing itself is culturally biased, and we agree, but we don't think there is any way that we are not going to have testing. What we can do is help our state educators vet the tests for obvious cultural biases, and we can help make this a constant, ongoing process.

Sixth, some will achieve "success" by teaching to the test. Oppose this publicly as unethical and unprofessional. Raise this issue in all kinds of settings. Try to get educators thinking about this, addressing it, criticizing the practice. The point of both standards and accountability is getting children to really learn, not to just pass the test. Most educators already understand this, so this is a strong point educators cannot easily ignore.

Seventh, there will be schools and districts that early on really start to improve, schools and districts that quickly take up this challenge and succeed. First, you will likely see individual schools, especially elementary schools, that are making significant strides toward equity and erasure of the achievement gap without sacrificing excellence. Then, two to four years in, you will start to see whole districts accomplishing this. Point out these examples. Visit them and see what they are doing. Help promote them. Help make them well known as exemplars; this will influence others within your state.

Eighth, because of the changes that will be instituted as a result of the NCLB, the use of data to make our decisions, to examine our schools, to understand where inequity exists, and to identify progress toward equity is only going to become more important. Thus, the equity audits that we have demonstrated here will be useful, as will Johnson's 2002 book. Working with data is just going to become a more typical aspect of our work as educators. Use it to increase equity.

Ninth, we will continue to see conversations on building the capacity of teachers in order to be successful with all children. We also hope we will see more conversation on building the capacity of leaders to facilitate the development of schools that serve all children well. Thus, professional development will grow in importance, but it will be professional development more focused on skills for succeeding with all children, and it will become more targeted at the specific needs of specific teachers or administrators who are having trouble being more successful with specific children or groups of children.

Tenth, the other areas we have covered in this small book, like leadership, parent and community involvement, and, hopefully, proactive redundancy will also grow in importance. One thing, though, that we can tell you for sure. The new focus on disaggregated data at your state level will, year by year, change the education conversation in your state, and we see this change as having numerous promising possibilities. We hope you can watch these changes and intervene at all levels to promote both equity and excellence, always the two together and never the two separate or set in conflict with each other.

FINAL WORDS, THE FINAL CALL

Thanks for listening to us. Thanks for caring about equity and excellence in schooling. We know of nothing more important in our public educational system than equity *and* excellence in every one of our classrooms, schools, and districts.

We believe that in this current historical moment we can make great strides toward both equity and excellence in schooling. We believe at this moment that we educators can make a really important difference that will be a great moment in our history.

This is our work. This is our commitment. This is our duty. This is our journey. It is our sacred democratic duty. It is our spiritual journey.

We are part of a long history of fellow citizens working to bring equity to our society. We stand on the shoulders of many wonderful, incredible people before us, people who took substantial risks to create what we now have. If we do the same, others will stand on our shoulders, honoring us, honoring children.

Who among us could ask for a better service, a better duty, a better journey? When our work is done, we will know that our mission, our journey, was a truly important one, a meaningful one, a deeply satisfying one.

However, right now, go to work, lead, get it done, collaboratively facilitate the development of classrooms, schools, and districts that are both equitable and excellent. Each and every child—no exceptions—must feel loved by us and must succeed academically. That is the call we are making. That is the call we hope you share with us.

May you have faith, the sustenance of colleagues on the same journey, and many successes, large and small.

References

American Federation of Teachers (AFT). (1999). *Making standards matter.* [Retrieved Feb. 13, 2003 from www.aft.org/edissues/standards99/toc.htm]

Artiles, A. J. (1998). The dilemma of difference: Enriching the disproportionality discourse with theory and context. *Journal of Special Education, 32*(1), 32-36.

Ashby, D. E. (2000, April). *The standards issue in preparing school leaders: Moving toward higher quality preparation and assessment.* Paper presented at the annual convention of the American Association of School Administrators, San Francisco.

Banks, J. A., Cookson, P., Gay, G., Hawley, W. D., Irvine, J. J., Nieto, S., Schofield, J. W., & Stephan, W. G. (2001). Diversity within unity: Essential principles for teaching and learning in a multicultural society. *Phi Delta Kappan, 83,* 196-202.

Bourdieu, P. (1982). The school as a conservative force: Scholastic and cultural inequalities. In E. Bredo & W. Feinberg (Eds.), *Knowledge and values in social and educational research* (pp. 391-407). Philadelphia: Temple University Press.

Bridge the gap: Schools must examine suspension policy. (1997, June 4). *Michigan Daily Online.* Retrieved December 31, 2002, from http://www.pub.umich.edu/daily/1997/jun/06-04-97/edit/edit1.html

California Department of Education. (n.d.). Grade one mathematics content standards. Retrieved December 31, 2002, from http://www.cde.ca.gov/standards/math/grade1.html

Capper, C. A., Keyes, M. A., & Frattura, E. (2000). *Meeting the needs of students of all abilities: How leaders go beyond inclusion.* Thousand Oaks, CA: Corwin.

Cawelti, G. (1999). *Portraits of six benchmark schools: Diverse approaches to improving student achievement.* Arlington, VA: Educational Research Service.

Chavez, C. (1968). Speech to migrant farm workers at Delano, California. Retrieved December 31, 2002, from http://www.sfsu.edu/%7Ececipp/cesar_chavez/statement.htm

Chavez, C. (1995). *Education of the heart: Cesar E. Chavez in his own words.* Retrieved December 31, 2002, from http://www.mit.edu/afs/athena/course/21/21f704/Chicano/CesarChavez Quotes.html

Cohen, D. K., & Hill, H. C. (2001). *Learning policy: When state education reform works.* New Haven, CT: Yale University Press.

Darling-Hammond, L., & Sclan, E. M. (1996). Who teaches and why: Dilemmas of building a profession for twenty-first century schools. In J. Sikula (Ed.), *Handbook of research on teacher education* (2nd ed., pp. 61-101). New York: Macmillan.

Delgado-Gaitan, C. (1992). School matters in the Mexican-American home: Socializing children into education. *American Educational Research Journal, 29,* 495-513.

Delpit, L. (1996). *Other people's children: Cultural conflict in the classroom.* New York: New Press.

Deschenes, S., Cuban, L., & Tyack, D. (2001). Mismatch: Historical perspectives on schools and students who don't fit them. *Teachers College Record, 103,* 525-548.

Devlin, B., Resnick, D. P., & Roeder, K. (Eds.). (1998). *Intelligence, genes, and success: Scientists respond to* The Bell Curve. New York: Copernicus.

Dewey, J. (1897). *My pedagogic creed.* Retrieved December 31, 2002, from http://www.infed.org/archives/e-texts/e-dew-pc.htm

Douglass, F. (1881). *Life and times of Frederick Douglass written by himself: His early life as a slave, his escape from bondage, and his complete history to the present time* [Electronic version]. Retrieved December 31, 2002, from http://docsouth.unc.edu/douglasslife/douglass.html

Eaker-Rich, D., & Van Galen, J. (1996). *Caring in an unjust world: Negotiating borders and barriers in schools.* Albany: State University of New York Press.

Edmonds, R. R. (1979). Effective schools for the urban poor. *Educational Leadership, 37*(1), 15-18, 20-24.

Edmonds, R. R. (1986). Characteristics of effective schools. In U. Neisser (Ed.), *The school achievement of minority children: New perspectives* (pp. 93-104). Hillsdale, NJ: Lawrence Erlbaum.

English, F. W., & Steffy, B. E. (2001). *Curriculum alignment: Creating a level playing field for all children on high-stakes tests of educational accountability.* Lanham, MD: Scarecrow Press.

Ferguson, R. F. (1998). Can schools narrow the Black-White test score gap. In C. Jencks & M. Phillips (Eds.), *The Black-White test score gap* (pp. 318-375). Washington, DC: Brookings Institution Press.

Ford, D. Y., & Harmon, D. A. (2001). Equity and excellence: Providing access to gifted education for culturally diverse students. *Journal of Secondary Gifted Education, 11,* 141-148.

Fox, S. J. (2001). *American Indian/Alaskan Native education and standards based reform.* (ERIC Digest EDO RC-01-2)

Fraser, S. (1995). *The Bell Curve wars: Race, intelligence, and the future of America.* New York: Perseus.

Gay, G. (2000). *Culturally responsive teaching: Theory, research, and practice.* New York: Teachers College Press.

Glickman, C. D. (2001). Dichotomizing education: Why no one wins and America loses. *Phi Delta Kappan, 83,* 147-152.

Glickman, C. D. (2002). *Leadership for learning: How to help teachers succeed.* Alexandria, VA: Association for Supervision and Curriculum Development.

Gonzalez, N., Moll, L. C., & Tenery, M. (1995). Funds of knowledge for teaching in Latino households. *Urban Education, 29,* 443-470.

Guajardo, M., Sanchez, P., Fineman, E., & Scheurich, J. J. (Writers/Directors/Producers). (1999). *The labors of life/ labores de la vida* [Video documentary]. (Available from Professor James Joseph Scheurich, Department of

Educational Administration, Sanchez 310, University of Texas at Austin, Austin, Texas 78712)

Haney, W. (2001). Response to Skrla et al. The illusion of educational equity in Texas: A commentary on "Accountability for Equity." *International Journal of Leadership in Education*, 4, 267-275.

Haycock, K. (2001). Closing the achievement gap. *Educational Leadership, 58*(6) 6-11 [electronic version].

Herrnstein, R. L., & Murray, C. (1996). *The bell curve: Intelligence and class structure in American life.* New York: Free Press.

Hollins, E. R. (1994). *Teaching diverse populations.* Albany: State University of New York Press.

Hollins, E. R., & Hernandez Sheets, R. (1999). *Racial and ethnic identity in school practices: Aspects of human development.* Mahwah, NJ: Lawrence Erlbaum.

Ingersoll, R. M. (1999). The problem of underqualified teachers in American secondary schools. *Educational Researcher, 28*(2), 26-37.

Jackson, J. H. (n.d.). *Message from the director.* Retrieved April 30, 2002, from http://www.naacp.org/work/education/edudirector.shtml

Johnson, R. (1996). *Setting our sights: Measuring equity in school change.* Los Angeles: Achieve.

Johnson, R. (2002). *Using data to close the achievement gap: How to measure equity in our schools.* Thousand Oaks, CA: Corwin.

Kincheloe, J. L, Steinberg, S. R., & Gresson, A. (1996). *Measured lies:* The Bell Curve *examined.* New York: Palgrave.

King, M. L. (1963). *I have a dream.* Retrieved December 31, 2002, from http://web66.coled.umn.edu/new/MLK/ MLK.html

King, M. L. (1967). *Beyond Vietnam: A time to break silence.* Retrieved December 31, 2002, from http://www.aquarianonline.com/Values/King.html

Klein, S. (2001). Response to Skrla et al.: Is there a connection between educational equity and accountability? *International Journal of Leadership in Education, 4,* 261-266.

Koschoreck, J. W. (2001). Accountability and educational equity in the transformation of an urban district. *Education and Urban Society, 33,* 284-305.

Kuykendall, C. (1992). *From rage to hope*. Bloomington, IN: National Educational Service.

Ladson-Billings, G. (1994). *The dreamkeepers: Successful teachers of African American children*. San Francisco: Jossey-Bass.

Lawler, E. E., Mohrman, S. A., & Benson, G. (2001). *Organizing for high performance: Employee involvement, TQM, reengineering, and knowledge management in the Fortune 1000*. San Francisco: Jossey-Bass.

Linn, R. L., Baker, E. L., & Betebenner, D. W. (2002). Accountability systems: Implications of requirements of the No Child Left Behind Act of 2001. *Educational Researcher, 31*(6), 3-16.

Linn, R. L., & Haug, C. (2002). Stability of school building scores and gains. *Educational Evaluation and Policy Analysis, 24*(1), 27-36.

Lopez, G. R., Scribner, J. D., & Mahitivanichcha, K. (2001). Redefining parental involvement: Lessons from high-performing migrant-impacted schools. *American Educational Research Journal, 38*, 253-288.

Loucks-Horsley, S., Hewson, P. W., Love, N., & Stiles, K. E. (1997). *Designing professional development for teachers of math and science*. Thousand Oaks, CA: Corwin.

Mankiller, W. (1993). *Rebuilding the Cherokee Nation*. Retrieved August 23, 2002, from http://gos.sbc.edu/m/mankiller.html

Marx, S. (2002, April). *Naming whiteness and white racism with white pre-service teachers: Empowerment through dialogue*. Paper presented at the annual meeting of the American Educational Research Association, New Orleans, LA.

McKenzie, K. (2002, April). *A school leader studies white teachers' perceptions of their students of color and of themselves as white educators*. Paper presented at the annual meeting of the American Educational Research Association, New Orleans, LA.

Meier, D. (2000). *Educating a democracy: Standards and the future of public education* [Electronic version]. Retrieved December 31, 2002, from http://bostonreview.mit.edu/BR24.6/meier.html

Mitchell, J. K., & Poston, W. K. (1992). The equity audit in school reform: Three case studies of educational disparity and incongruity. *International Journal of Educational Reform, 1*, 242-247.

Moll, L. C. (1992). Bilingual classroom studies and community analysis: Some recent trends. *Educational Researcher, 20*(2), 20-24.

Moses, R., & Cobb, C. E., Jr. (2002). *Radical equations: Math literacy and civil rights*. Boston: Beacon.

Noddings, N. (1986). *Caring: A feminine approach to ethics and moral education*. Berkeley: University of California Press.

Noddings, N. (1992). *The challenge to care in schools: An alternative approach to education*. New York: Teachers College Press.

Paige, R. (2002). *Welcome letter*. Retrieved March 5, 2002, from http://www.NoChildLeftBehind.gov/start/welcome/index.html

Pappas, G., & Lucero, M. G. (1995-1996). Colorado's community speaks out about school discipline legislation that impacts the Latino. *Harvard Journal of Hispanic Policy, 9*, 87-112.

Price, H. B. (2001). The preparation gap: Eliminate it first, then the achievement gap. *Education Week*. [Retrieved Feb. 13, 2003, www.edweek.org]

Prince, C. D. (2002). *The challenge of attracting good teachers and principals to struggling schools*. Retrieved December 31, 2002, from http://www.aasa.org/issues_and_insights/issues_dept/challenges.htm

Reyes, P., Scribner, J. D., & Paredes Scribner, A. (1999). *Lessons from high-performing Hispanic schools: Creating learning communities*. New York: Teachers College Press.

Riester, A. F., Pursch, V., & Skrla, L. (2002). Principals for social justice: Leaders of school success for children from low-income homes. *Journal of School Leadership, 12*, 281-304.

Sanders, W. L., & Rivers, J. C. (1996). *Cumulative and residual effects of teachers on future student academic achievement*. Knoxville: University of Tennessee Value-Added Research and Assessment Center.

Scheurich, J. J. (1998). Highly successful and loving public elementary schools populated mainly by low SES children of color: Core beliefs and cultural characteristics. *Urban Education, 33,* 451-491.

Scheurich, J. J., & Skrla, L. (2001). Continuing the conversation on equity and accountability. *Phi Delta Kappan, 83,* 322-326.

Scheurich, J. J., Skrla, L., & Johnson, J. F. (2000). Thinking carefully about equity and accountability. *Phi Delta Kappan, 82,* 293-299.

Scott, B. (2001, March). Coming of age. *IDRA Newsletter.* Retrieved December 31, 2002, from http://www.idra.org/Newslttr/2001/Mar/Bradley.htm

Senge, P. M. (1990). *The fifth discipline.* New York: Doubleday.

Sergiovanni, T. J. (1994). *Building community in schools.* San Francisco: Jossey-Bass.

Skrla, L., Garcia, J., Scheurich, J. J., & Nolly, G. (2002, April). *Educational equity profiles: Practical leadership tools for equitable and excellent schools.* Paper presented at the annual meeting of the American Educational Research Association, New Orleans, LA.

Skrla, L., Scheurich, J. J., & Johnson, J. F. (Eds.). (2001). Accountability and achievement in high poverty school settings [Special issue]. *Education and Urban Society, 33*(3).

Skrla, L., Scheurich, J. J., & Johnson, J. F. (2000). *Equity-driven, achievement-focused school districts: A report on systemic school success in four Texas school districts serving diverse populations.* Retrieved December 31, 2002, from http://www.utdanacenter.org/research/reports/equitydistricts.pdf

Skrla, L., Scheurich, J. J., Johnson, J. F., & Koschoreck, J. W. (2001a). Accountability for equity: Can state policy leverage social justice? *International Journal of Leadership in Education, 4,* 237-260.

Skrla, L., Scheurich, J. J., Johnson, J. F., & Koschoreck, J. W. (2001b). Complex and contested constructions of accountability and educational equity. *International Journal of Leadership in Education, 4,* 277-283.

Spillane, J. P., Halverson, R., & Diamond, J. B. (2001). Investigating school leadership practice: A distributed perspective. *Educational Researcher, 30*(3), 23-38.

Spirituality in Leadership [Special issue]. (2002, September). *School Administrator.* Retrieved December 31, 2002, from http://www.aasa.org/publications/sa/2002_09/contents.htm

Texas Education Agency. (1997). Texas Administrative Code, Title 19, Part II, Chapter 111. Texas Essential Knowledge and Skills for Mathematics. Retrieved from http://www.tea.state.tx.us/rules/tac/chapter111/ch111a.pdf

Townsend, B. L. (2000). The disproportionate discipline of African American learners. *Exceptional Children, 66,* 381-392.

U.S. Department of Education. (2002). *No child left behind act of 2001: Executive summary.* Retrieved December 31, 2002, from http://www.ed.gov/offices/OESE/esea/exec-summ.html

Valencia, R. R. (1997). *The evolution of deficit thinking.* London: Falmer.

Valencia, R. R. (2000). *Intelligence testing and minority students.* Thousand Oaks, CA: Sage.

Valencia, R. R., Valenzuela, A., Sloan, K., & Foley, D. E. (2001). Let's treat the cause, not the symptoms: Equity and accountability in Texas revisited. *Phi Delta Kappan, 83,* 318-321.

Valenzuela, A. (1999). *Subtractive schooling: U.S.-Mexican youth and the politics of caring.* Albany: State University of New York Press.

Young, M. D. (1998, April). *Importance of trust in increasing parental involvement and student achievement in Mexican American communities.* Paper presented at the annual meeting of the American Educational Research Association, San Diego, CA. (ERIC Document Reproduction Service No. ED423587)

Index

**CORWIN
PRESS**

The Corwin Press logo—a raven striding across an open book—
represents the happy union of courage and learning. We are a
professional-level publisher of books and journals for K-12 educators,
and we are committed to creating and providing resources that
embody these qualities. Corwin's motto is "Success for All Learners."